Seeing
RED

'I've given you fair warning, Victoria,' shouted Dad, 'but you've chosen consistently to go against me.'

'You shouldn't be such a bully!' shouted Vicky. 'I hate you! You're the worst father ever!'

'And you're the very worst daughter! You don't give a damn, do you?'

'Nor do you!'

'I won't stand for it any longer! V⟩   ⟩ria, you've gone too far. If you can't or *won't* change your ways and keep to our rules, I've a good mind to throw   ⟩'

Seeing Red
by Jill Atkins

Published by Ransom Publishing Ltd.
Radley House, 8 St. Cross Road, Winchester, Hampshire SO23 9HX, UK
www.ransom.co.uk

ISBN   978 178127 663 1
First published in 2001
This revised edition published in 2015

Seeing RED

JILL ATKINS

Ransom

Chapter
ONE

Vicky Brown gently pushed her key into the lock and turned it. She held her breath as the door slowly swung open then she stepped into the hall, closing the door behind her as softly as she could. All quiet. She relaxed a little. Her parents were probably in bed. She began to tiptoe towards the stairs.

'Victoria!'

Her dad's harsh voice made her jump. She stopped dead, her heart hammering inside her chest. Dad stormed into the hall, his face dark with anger.

'Where have you been?' he demanded, pulling his

sleeve up and tapping his watch. 'Don't you know what time it is?'

Vicky shrugged her shoulders as her mum came and stood beside Dad.

'It's almost midnight,' he said. 'Too late for a girl of your age to be out.'

'No, it's not!'

'Don't argue!'

'We thought you were being brought home at ten,' said Mum.

'I was,' said Vicky. 'But it didn't work out.'

'Why not?' asked Mum.

'Sarah's sick so she didn't come out, and her mum was our lift. We had to make our own way home.'

'You should have rung,' said Dad.

'Oh, stop making such a fuss!' said Vicky. 'I'm here now, aren't I?'

'Don't you realise how worried we've been?' Mum asked quietly. 'We've been frantic, haven't we, Richard?'

Vicky's dad nodded. 'I've been out in the car looking for you,' he said. 'Up and down the streets so many times I got stopped by the police. They thought I looked suspicious.'

Vicky sniggered. To think they thought *that* of her dad!

'It's no laughing matter,' said Dad. 'Anything could have happened to you. You were supposed to be in two hours ago.'

'Get real, Dad. It's no big deal. I've already told you, Sarah's mum wasn't there … and we forgot the time.'

'That's no excuse!' said Dad. 'We bought you a decent watch … '

' … which I wasn't wearing.'

He took a step towards her. 'You're a selfish, ungrateful girl. This isn't the first time you've defied us, is it? Last night you were half an hour late. Last week, it was nearly an hour. If we say you should be home by ten o'clock, we mean ten o'clock.'

'But ten's so ridiculously early,' Vicky protested. 'Lizzie … '

'I don't care about Lizzie,' said Dad. 'It's *you* we care about.'

'No, you don't,' said Vicky. 'If you *really* cared about me, you'd let me stay out a lot later. Anyway, I was quite safe.'

'How could we know that?' asked Dad. 'Where were you, anyway?'

7

'At Josh's.'

'Oh … well, why didn't you let us know?'

Vicky shrugged her shoulders again.

'You've blown it this time.' The voice came from upstairs.

Vicky looked up. Her brother, Matt, was leaning over the banisters with a big grin across his face.

'Shut up, creep!' she shouted.

'Keep out of this, Matthew!' snapped Dad.

'You let *him* stay out late!' shouted Vicky, pointing at her brother.

'He doesn't go out as often as you.'

'That's because he's such a swot,' said Vicky.

'And he's two years older than you,' said Mum. 'And he's a boy.'

Vicky thought her head would explode. What had she done to be landed with such old-fashioned, narrow-minded parents?

'You're so sexist!' she yelled.

'That's enough, Victoria!' shouted Dad. 'You've done this once too often, so I've made up my mind. You're not going out in the evenings until you learn to come home at a reasonable time.'

'You can't stop me!'

'Oh yes I can … and I will!'

'How can you be so mean?' she yelled.

She stormed up the stairs, pushing Matt out of her way, and rushed into her bedroom, slamming the door and locking it behind her. Then she flung herself down on her bed. Almost immediately, she heard thundering footsteps on the stairs and then the door handle being rattled.

'Victoria!' Dad shouted, hammering on the door. 'Open up, this minute!'

Vicky lifted her pillow and pulled it down over her head. She couldn't bear to listen to her dad any longer.

'Victoria!' She could still hear his harsh voice through the pillow. 'Come out here and apologise.'

'Fat chance!' Vicky muttered to herself. 'You've got another thing coming if you're hoping for an apology. For what? For having mean parents who stop me doing *anything*?'

'Vicky.' Her mother's voice was quieter, pleading. 'Please open this door and let's all try and sort things out. Come on, Vicky. Be sensible.'

'Sensible?' Vicky muttered. 'What's sensible about this entire, miserable world, I want to know!'

She lifted the pillow and sat up.

'I'm not coming out,' she said, 'so you might as well go away and leave me alone.'

'But, Vicky … ' said her mum.

'You're too soft on her, Lin,' she heard her dad say. 'She needs a firm hand. Victoria, you're only fifteen.'

'Nearly sixteen!'

'You need to learn that we mean what we say.'

Vicky sighed. It was always the same. *Vicky this, Vicky that,* the story of her life. Never *Matt this, Matt that,* except when she was hearing how marvellous he was.

Suddenly, there was a loud wailing sound.

'Now look what you've done!' shouted Dad. 'You've woken Katie.'

Vicky seethed. 'It's not me doing all the shouting!'

It always seemed to be *her* fault if her little sister cried. She heard her mum quietening Katie, then after a while she heard her dad go downstairs. They had given up nagging her for the moment, but she guessed it would not end there.

Bruno was lying on the end of her bed. She picked him up and held him in front of her face. She had had him since she was born and although the little

bear was rather battered and dirty, he was still one of
her favourite possessions. She quietly hugged him
until she felt calmer then she put him on the bed,
took her mobile phone from her bag and called
Lizzie. It rang for quite a long time.

'Hi,' said a sleepy voice.

'Hi,' said Vicky. 'Sorry, are you in bed?'

'Yeah, just gone to sleep.' Lizzie yawned. 'What
d'you want?'

'I've had enough!'

'Why? What's up?'

'I've been grounded.'

'Oh no! That's terrible! Why?'

'Why do you think? By the time I got home after
leaving you, I was almost two hours late. And you
know my Dad. He always wants me in by ten. Well
… he went ballistic.'

'What about your mum?'

'Oh, you know what she's like – much quieter, but
she's on Dad's side. They've ganged up against me.'

'What happened?'

'We had a massive row, then Katie went and woke
up and I got the blame, as usual! It really cheeses me
off. Things have been so different around here since

she was born. I always have to keep quiet in case I wake her up.'

'But she's only four,' said Lizzie.

'So? She's so spoilt. She gets everything she wants … and she always has to win games or she might throw a tantrum and … '

'But she's so cute and pretty.'

'That's what everyone thinks. But *I* know what she's really like.'

'Poor old you.'

'They never get off my back. It's hell living here. I'm never allowed to have my own opinion about anything, unless it agrees with my parents. They're always right and I'm always wrong.'

'What are you going to do?'

'I don't know.' Vicky felt tears welling up in her eyes. 'I sometimes think they'd be better off without me.'

'Don't do anything stupid,' said Lizzie. 'Ring me again in the morning.'

'OK. Sorry I rambled on. Thanks for listening, Lizzie. Night.'

'Night.'

Vicky wiped her eyes and blew her nose hard.

Then she got undressed, climbed into bed and put out her light. Tomorrow she would think more clearly about what she was going to do.

Chapter
TWO

As soon as Vicky woke next morning, she put a disc in her CD player and turned it on. The music burst out and she tapped her foot to the deep, pulsing rhythm. She closed her eyes and nodded her head to the beat. Yes! She could blow all thoughts of gross parents clean away.

At that moment there was a thumping sound, even louder than the beat of the music.

'Turn that row down!' Matt's voice came through the door. 'I'm trying to work.'

Vicky turned a knob and the volume increased. That would teach Matthew creep-a-lot Brown not to be such a boffin.

'I've got exams in a few weeks,' Matt yelled, banging again. 'So have you, for that matter. Or does a little thing like that escape your memory?'

Vicky shuddered. Exams! Homework! School! They all stink! Who needs to pass exams anyway? It's all a waste of time.

'You're mad!' she shouted back. '*I'm* not doing homework on a Saturday.'

'You won't pass anything at that rate!'

'See if I care!'

Vicky cut the sound mid-track. Not that she had turned it off for her brother's sake, of course. She was hungry. She was going to breeze downstairs for breakfast and see what kind of mood everyone was in. Perhaps if she made the effort to be nice to them all, Dad would change his mind, for once.

'Morning, Vicky,' said Mum, who was in the kitchen giving Katie her cereal. 'Did you sleep well?'

'OK, I suppose,' Vicky muttered. She made herself some toast and tea.

Katie started grizzling. 'I don't want cereal,' she complained. 'I want toast.'

Vicky frowned, but gave Katie some of her toast and sat down at the table. Her dad was reading the paper. After a moment, he put the paper down, drank his tea then looked up.

'Morning, Vicky,' he said.

Vicky forced a smile. 'Morning,' she said. Her dad seemed to be in quite a good mood. She sipped her tea then took a deep breath. 'I don't suppose you could change your mind about tonight?' she asked. 'Only I've arranged to go to a disco with Lizzie.'

'So you'll have to ring Lizzie and tell her you can't come.'

'*Dad!* Please! I know I've been late and I'm sorry, but couldn't you give me one more chance. I'll really try and be home on time. *Please!*'

Her dad frowned, got up and went to stand by the back door.

'All right,' he said after a moment. 'I suppose so. You can have one last chance. Just show us how responsible you can be, for once. In by eleven.'

'Eleven? But … '

'Take it or leave it,' said Dad.

'OK. OK.'

'And I'll come and pick you up.'

'No, Josh's dad is fetching us.'

'Well, he'd better be more reliable than Sarah's

mum,' said Dad, as he stepped outside. 'Have you got his number? I'll ring him.'

Vicky dashed back upstairs to her room, humming. It was time to ring Lizzie.

Just before seven o'clock that evening, Vicky sat down in front of her mirror.

'Cinderella,' she said, with a big grin. 'You *shall* go to the ball!'

She carefully made up her face. The black eye shadow and purple lipstick did things for her, went really well with the silver nose ring and the stark dark hair. When she was satisfied with her appearance, she slung her black jacket over her shoulders and opened her bedroom door. As she crept past Matt's room she peered in at him. He was sitting bent over his table with his back to her.

'Where you going?' he asked quietly.

Vicky jumped. He must have very good hearing to have known she was there.

'Out,' she said.

Matt turned round. 'Hey, you look a sight!'

'Thanks!'

'I thought you were grounded.'

'You don't know everything, do you? Dad's changed his mind.'

'You jammy devil! Well, keep out of trouble.'

'Stop sounding like a boring old fart,' said Vicky.

'Oh, I give up,' said Matt, turning back to his book. 'Do what you like.'

What a creep! Vicky was just about to leave him to it when his voice stopped her dead.

'Did you bunk off school again yesterday?'

'No!' Vicky glared at the back of his head. How did he know? She thought she had managed to keep it a secret.

'Don't deny it. Everyone knows you did.'

Everyone? 'Not Mum and Dad?'

'You want to watch it,' he said. 'School will be ringing home if you keep doing it. Then *they'll* find out, but it won't be me that tells on you. I'd rather not have to put up with any more rows!'

'Ta, Matt.' He wasn't so bad, as brothers go, but she'd have to be careful. If her parents found out, World War Three would erupt!

She went round for Lizzie. Lizzie was lucky. Her mum and step-dad didn't care where she went or what she

18

did or when she got in. They were too busy having a good time.

'So you made it,' said Lizzie when she opened the door to Vicky. 'How did you persuade them to let you out?'

'Just my charm!' said Vicky with a grin. 'You ready?'

'Five minutes,' said Lizzie.

They went up to Lizzie's room, passing her mum on the landing.

'Going somewhere nice?' she asked.

'Disco,' said Lizzie.

'Have a great time.'

Ten minutes later they were walking in the warm light evening to meet the others at the flat where Josh lived with his dad.

'Hey, why weren't you at school yesterday?' asked another friend called Julie, when Vicky and Lizzie squashed with about ten others into the small kitchen. 'Old Smokey made a comment about you being an invisible student.'

Vicky grinned then pulled a face.

'What's the point of going to school?' she said. 'It's

so boring. So there's GCSEs coming up. Big deal. I wouldn't get any decent grades if I tried, so I've decided I'm going to skip them. Anyway, I'll be sixteen in a few weeks. I'm going to leave school on my sixteenth birthday.'

'Hey, you two!' said Lizzie. 'Lay off that dreaded subject, will you? We're trying hard to forget all that, aren't we?'

By the time they left the flat and made for the disco, Vicky felt ready for anything. She was determined to forget school and home and enjoy herself. As soon as they arrived at Rizzi's, she went straight in, pushing her way onto the crowded dance floor. Dancing – she loved it! The flashing lights and the boom of the beat took her over. She was blind and deaf to everything else. This was living!

She danced with Lizzie or Sarah mostly and several times with Josh, then on her own. She suddenly felt thirsty, and was at the bar buying a cola when Lizzie came up and shouted in her ear.

'Josh's dad will be here soon. We'll have to leave in a couple of minutes.'

Vicky could barely hear against the volume of the music.

'What, already?' she shouted. 'I've only just got into my stride.'

Ten minutes later, Vicky was back in the middle of the dance floor when Lizzie came up to her again.

'Come on,' Lizzie yelled. 'Josh's dad must be outside waiting by now.'

'Be with you in a sec,' shouted Vicky and turned her back on her friend.

'*Vicky!*'

Vicky whipped round. 'What?'

'We've got to go. *Now!*'

'God! You can be so bossy! You're beginning to sound just like my dad!'

'Thanks very much! And you're becoming a right pain these days!'

'Pain, is it?' yelled Vicky. 'Well, thanks for nothing!'

A few metres away she saw another couple of friends from school. Jane and Becky were OK.

'I wouldn't dream of offending you with my presence any longer,' she yelled at Lizzie. 'I'll go home with Jane and Becky.'

She danced over to the two girls.

'All right if I cadge a lift with you?' she shouted.

21

Becky nodded. 'No problem!'

Vicky lost all idea of time as the music went on and on. Suddenly, she noticed that the crowd had thinned. She peered at her watch. Way past eleven! Oh no! How could the time have gone so quickly? She looked around for Jane and Becky, but they weren't there. She found her jacket and made for the exit. Perhaps they were waiting for her outside.

But they had gone. Cursing her so-called friends, Vicky stood on the steps of Rizzi's and stared up and down the street. It was quiet and dark and empty. She daren't go out there alone. It was spooky. What was she going to do?

She cursed herself for being so stupid.

Why didn't I go home with Lizzie and Josh, as planned? I must have had some kind of brainstorm. Perhaps I should ring Dad … No. I refuse to grovel and beg him for a lift. Anyway, I can't bear the thought of him yelling at me down the phone. He'll be livid. He'll say I've let them down and I've only got myself to blame, which I suppose is true. He won't forgive me this time. I'll have to creep in again and hope they've gone to bed. But I haven't got any money for a cab. How am I going to get home?

Suddenly, she had a brilliant idea. Uncle Tom! He only lived a few streets away. He always stayed up late. You wouldn't guess that he and her dad were brothers. He was so easy going. He wouldn't mind.

Pulling her jacket around her, she stepped out into the dark night. The deep shadows between the street lamps along the road didn't look very inviting, but she had no choice. She would have to risk it. Keeping near the kerb, she began to walk as quickly and as quietly as she could, but each step seemed to echo and she stopped several times to listen and peer into the darkness.

There was a sound behind her. Was someone following her? She daren't turn round. Her legs began to shake as she broke into a run. It seemed like miles to her uncle's house, but somehow she covered the distance at a record speed. She arrived panting on the doorstep. His light was on. She rang the bell.

'Who is it?' Tom asked from behind the closed door.

'Vicky.'

The door opened immediately. He stepped back to let her in.

'What are you doing here at this time of night?'

Vicky told him what had happened.

'I'm in big trouble with dad because I'm late again,' she said. 'And I'm dead scared of the dark. So I was wondering if you'd mind walking me home?'

Tom grinned. 'All right,' he said. 'As long as you don't want me to take your side against my big brother!'

As they set off, Vicky linked arms with her uncle, her fear gone. She felt safe, but she didn't want to talk. She was feeling very nervous about arriving home. Would she be able to sneak in unnoticed? Or would her father be waiting for her?

After twenty minutes brisk walking, she could just make out the house in the distance. The lights were still on. Her stomach began to churn with nerves.

'I always manage to get myself into trouble,' she said. 'I sometimes think they'd all be happier if I wasn't there.'

'Don't be silly,' said Uncle Tom.

'I suppose there's no chance I could come and live with you?' she asked.

Tom laughed. 'Absolutely no chance!' he said.

'Will you at least come in with me now?'

'No, Vicky. It's between you and your dad. This is where I leave you.'

Vicky stood at the front gate and watched her Uncle Tom trot back along the road. Then she found her key, guessing she was about to face the biggest row ever.

Chapter
THREE

The front door swung violently open. Vicky's dad stood towering above her with an angry scowl on his face.

'Get inside, you deceitful girl!' he shouted. 'You need to explain yourself.'

'Why? I went to the disco,' Vicky shouted back defiantly as she stepped into the hall. 'You know that.'

'Don't be so rude!' he shouted as he slammed the door behind her.

'I'm not being rude. I'm tired and fed up. I had to walk home again.'

'Don't tell such lies.'

'It's not lies! I did walk!'

'Are all your friends' parents that unreliable? If I'd come for you like I suggested, we wouldn't have had all this hassle. I've been trying to ring you, but your mobile must have been switched off. So I rang Josh's dad. Josh was home. He said you'd arranged a lift with a girl called Becky.'

'I did,' muttered Vicky crossly. 'But she went without me.'

'So why didn't you ring?'

'I thought you'd be angry.'

'Angry!' bellowed her dad. 'Of course I'd be angry. But I'm even madder now. You're not only rude and disobedient, but stupid as well.'

'Stupid?'

'Walking alone through the dark streets at this time of night! You know there are dangers … '

'I didn't,' shouted Vicky.

'Didn't what?'

'Didn't walk on my own. Uncle Tom brought me home.'

'Tom? What's my brother got to do with this? You didn't meet him at the disco, did you?'

Vicky laughed, though she felt more like crying.

She felt very tired and she had not quite recovered from the shock of her friends letting her down, or the fear she had felt as she left the disco alone.

'What's so funny?' asked her mum, who was standing at the living room door.

'Uncle Tom? At a disco?' Vicky said through her laughter, though she was desperately fighting off the tears. 'It wasn't for geriatrics, you know!'

'Then how did he manage to bring you home?' Dad shouted, even louder than before.

'I ran round to his flat and asked him, that's how!'

Matt appeared from the kitchen with a smirk on his face.

'Stop looking so pleased with yourself!' Vicky shouted.

'I'm not!' said Matt.

'Yes, you are. You're gloating. It makes you feel great to see me in trouble. Go on, admit it.'

'Oh, I give up!' said Matt.

'So why aren't you in bed?' Vicky snapped. 'Isn't it past your bedtime? You need your sleep to help that brain of yours to get you through your exams.'

'So do you,' said Matt. 'Your GCSEs are just as important as my A levels.'

'You're such a loser!'

'Don't be nasty, Vicky,' said Mum.

'I can't help it,' said Vicky, knowing she was about to blubber. 'You're all against me. It's not fair.'

'Oh, I can't stand this,' said Matt. 'I'm living in a lunatic asylum. I'm going to bed.'

He ran up the stairs and closed his bedroom door with a bang.

'Why do you have to be like this, Vicky?' cried Mum. 'You've managed to upset the whole family now. I wish you were as considerate as your brother and as sweet as your sister.'

'Oh, thanks!' shouted Vicky.

'You've turned into a bad-tempered, disobedient girl,' said her dad. 'I don't know what we're going to do with you. I gave you another chance, but you ruined it. You'll stay in from now on.'

'You're so horrible,' cried Vicky, bursting into tears. 'You used to understand me, but now all you want to do is make my life a misery.'

She dashed up to her room and sat on her bed, her throbbing head in her hands, wondering what to do. She felt wounded, empty, unloved. She picked up Bruno and hugged him.

'Why do they think Matt's so marvellous?' she muttered. 'Just because he doesn't argue and he's clever at school? Why do they spoil Katie something rotten? Can't they see what she's really like? And why do they treat me so unfairly?'

She held Bruno up in front of her face.

'Who can I talk to? Nobody. Uncle Tom refuses to get involved. Matt treats me like an alien. Katie's too young to understand. Mum's too pathetic to stand up against Dad. As for him, why has he changed so much lately? He used to be great fun, but now I've grown up he's become so strict. He doesn't understand me at all.'

Bruno's little button eyes stared back at her.

'And what about Lizzie? I thought she was my friend, but she says I'm a pain. Sarah and Josh and the others are all right, but I don't think they really care either.'

Next morning Vicky's loneliness had not gone away. After a restless night, she woke with a bad head and a bad mood to go with it. Her brain hurt from trying to sort out what she was going to do.

At about nine o'clock her mum knocked on her

door and came in with a cup of tea and some toast. She put them down on Vicky's dressing table and said, 'Morning, Vicky,' but she didn't look Vicky in the eye and left the room immediately.

Vicky drank the tea and nibbled at the toast, but she wasn't feeling hungry.

At that moment, her phone rang. She picked it up. 'Hi?'

'Did you get home all right last night?' It was Lizzie.

'No, I didn't.' Vicky was livid. 'You've got a cheek asking me that, leaving me in the lurch … '

'I didn't! I *told* you we had to go.'

'You could have waited a bit.'

'But … we did wait … for ages, until Josh's dad got mad and said he'd leave us if we didn't hurry up. Anyway, you said Becky and Jane … '

'They abandoned me.'

'So what did you do?'

'I had to walk,' said Vicky crossly. 'I was petrified.'

'Oh,' said Lizzie.

Vicky couldn't be bothered to tell her about the journey home or the row waiting for her when she arrived.

'S'OK,' she said. 'I forgive you.'

She rang off. She had said it, but she wasn't quite sure whether she meant it. She still felt betrayed.

There was a tap at the door and her mum poked her head into the room.

'Was that Lizzie?' she said.

'Yes,' Vicky muttered. 'Since when did you start eavesdropping on my phone calls?'

'Oh, Vicky.' Mum sighed then closed the door and went downstairs.

It seemed a long day, shut up in her room, but she didn't want to go down and face them. She ate nothing, even though Matt brought her a sandwich at lunchtime and her mum brought her a plate of dinner later on. Her dad had not been near her. By seven o'clock she was feeling stir-crazy.

'I've got to get out,' she muttered to herself in the mirror. 'Just for a while.'

But her mum and dad were both downstairs and it would not be easy getting past them. She stood looking out of the window. A lot of people were out. There always were on a Sunday night. It made her imprisonment even worse to see them there.

Why should she stay in? Her dad had no right to stop her going out.

She opened the window and peered down at the garage roof. That part should be easy, then it was only a short drop to the ground. She wouldn't be long – she had to try and sort things out with Lizzie.

Chapter
FOUR

Vicky did her hair, made up her face and changed
her clothes. Then she locked her bedroom door on
the inside, climbed out onto the garage roof and
jumped down onto the driveway. In a few minutes
she was knocking on Lizzie's door.

'I'm really sorry about last night,' said Lizzie as
soon as she let Vicky in. 'But I did keep telling you to
come.'

Vicky nodded. She'd been stupid, she realised
that. If she'd gone home with Josh's dad as planned
she would have been on time and she wouldn't have
been grounded. Why had she stayed late? She

couldn't answer that, except she suspected it might have something to do with wanting to get at her dad. But it had backfired badly.

They sat in Lizzie's kitchen over a cup of tea. For a while, neither of them spoke. Vicky began to wish she hadn't come. This was getting nowhere. But she needed someone to talk to. If she couldn't confide in Lizzie, who else was there?

'They won't change their minds this time,' she said miserably. 'I'm definitely grounded.'

'So how … ?'

'I sneaked out of my window.'

Lizzie gasped then laughed. 'Wow!'

'What do you think I should do?'

'I don't know. It's different for me. I don't have parent trouble.'

'I feel like leaving home,' said Vicky. 'I can't stand living there a moment longer.'

'But where would you go?'

'London, maybe. I could get work.'

'Don't go,' said Lizzie.

'I might,' said Vicky.

'You're seriously thinking of leaving school when you're sixteen?'

'Yep. Can't wait for my birthday. Then you won't see me for dust in that dump.'

Lizzie frowned. 'I wish you wouldn't,' she said. 'You'd regret it.'

Vicky suddenly didn't feel in the mood. Lizzie was sounding like the others, all trying to tell her what was best for her. She stood up.

'See you around,' she said.

She walked slowly home. She had been right. Lizzie didn't really understand. No one did. She was on her own.

She moved the dustbin to the side of the garage and climbed up into her bedroom. It seemed nobody had noticed she'd been out. She turned on her music and put her earphones on, drowning her misery. If anyone knocked on her door, she certainly didn't hear them. She felt isolated, lost in a world of strangers.

For the next two weeks she was grounded in the evenings. She knew she could escape by her secret route any time she liked, but somehow she couldn't be bothered. She spent her time listening to her CDs, playing them with the volume at mind-bending heights. She went to school a few times, but she had loads of hassle from the staff. Even her so-called best friends only spoke to her when they had to. How could everything change so suddenly?

Then, one Saturday morning, her dad summoned her downstairs. She knew there was something up when she imagined she could see steam coming out of his ears. They went into the dining room and sat at the table with Vicky opposite her parents. It was like being in the dock in a courtroom.

A letter had arrived. It was from the Head. Dad's hand was shaking as he held up the letter.

'You've got some explaining to do,' he said, speaking very quietly. 'How dare you miss school! Your mother and I ... ' He waved the letter in front of Vicky's face. 'Fancy a daughter of ours ... I feel quite ashamed ... listen to this: *"Your daughter's future depends on her attending school and doing well in her exams"*. It goes on, *"Please ensure that she attends all next week. In addition, I cannot stress enough the importance of home study in the last two weeks before the exams start."* What are you thinking of, you stupid girl? Can't you see that your entire future could be mapped out for you if you do well in your GCSEs?'

'Just like Matt, you mean?'

'Well, you said it,' said Dad. 'Just like Matt.'

'You always compare me with him.' Vicky was beginning to feel her anger rising again. 'But I'm not him. I'm different. I'm me.'

Before he could reply, she dashed back upstairs. The case was closed.

Once the exams started, she had planned to steer clear of school altogether, but her parents took her in by car. She found herself having to sit the exams after all.

What hurt her most was that none of her friends rang or texted or even emailed her in the evenings. So she didn't contact them either. Why should she make the effort when they couldn't be bothered? She spent her non-exam days alone, hanging around at home or in the park or in the local coffee bar.

But the rows went on at home. She always managed to do something to annoy her parents or Matt or Katie. Her mood grew blacker and blacker. The whole world was against her.

On the morning of her birthday, she was surprised when the postman delivered cards from Lizzie and

Sarah, from her mum's old Aunt Sheila, and one from her grandma with twenty pounds tucked inside. On the breakfast table, she found three more cards, from Matt, Katie and Uncle Tom. She opened them all, but the usual birthday excitement was missing. She'd thought she would feel different, being sixteen, but she just stared at her cards as she put them in a pile.

'And here's one from your dad and me,' said Mum, giving her an envelope.

After breakfast, she followed Vicky upstairs and put some money on her bed.

'Don't tell your father,' she said. 'He'd kill me if he knew. He says you don't deserve anything, but I'm sure you can make use of this. Buy some new clothes.'

'Thanks,' Vicky said without a smile.

And that was that. The day passed like any other day. Nothing was said about celebrating her birthday. All her friends had had big parties on their sixteenth, so had Matt, but there was no chance she would get the same. In the evening, she went to her room as usual. At eight o'clock, she faced her reflection in the mirror.

'I've had enough!' she said. 'I'm going out!'

Locking her door and leaving her window ajar, she climbed out and headed for Lizzie's.

'Oh, hi,' said Lizzie. 'Happy birthday! Did they let you out for once?'

'No, they don't know,' said Vicky. 'I'll be out as late as I like and they won't even know I've gone.'

'Come on, then. What are we waiting for?'

But when Vicky was dropped off by the gang several hours later, with feet tired from dancing and a head sore from the heavy beat of the music, her window was shut.

'Damn,' she whispered, as she climbed down from the garage roof. 'They must have discovered my escape route!'

Desperately tired and dying for a good long sleep, she headed for the front door, but when she got there she found her dad on the step, seething with anger.

'That's it!' he yelled.

'Shh!' said Mum, pulling Vicky into the hall and shutting the door behind her.

'I've had it up to here with you!' yelled her dad. 'I never thought I could have fathered such a rebellious, ungrateful, revolting creature as you.'

Vicky refused to look at him. The sight of him made her sick.

'You blatantly disobey me time and time again,' he yelled at fever pitch. 'The trouble with you is you've got no respect.'

Vicky groaned. 'But it's my birthday.'

'That's got nothing to do with it, young madam, so your mother and I have made up our minds.'

'But ... ' said her mum.

Matt came down the stairs, half-asleep. 'What's going on?'

'Nothing, dear,' said Mum. 'Only Vicky in late.'

'Not again!'

'I've given you fair warning, Victoria,' shouted Dad, 'but you've chosen consistently to go against me.'

'You shouldn't be such a bully!' shouted Vicky. 'I hate you! You're the worst father ever!'

'And you're the very worst daughter! You don't give a damn, do you?'

'Nor do you!'

'I won't stand for it any longer!'

'But, Richard ... '

'Be quiet, Lin,' he yelled in her mum's face. 'We have to stand firm.'

'Don't say anything you'll regret,' cried Mum, her lip trembling. 'Be careful!'

'Be careful?' shouted Dad. 'It's too late for that. Victoria, you've gone too far. If you can't or *won't* change your ways and keep to our rules, I've a good mind to throw you out!'

'But where can she go?' cried Mum, tears streaming down her cheeks.

'She seems to enjoy going where she likes and doing what she wants,' shouted Dad. Then he turned on Vicky. 'Now get out of my sight!'

Chapter
FIVE

Vicky felt as if she had gone the distance in a kick-boxing bout. The shock of her dad's ultimatum had taken her breath away. Had he actually thrown her out? It certainly seemed like it. What else could he have meant? 'Get out of my sight!' he had shouted. That must mean she had to leave.

Stunned, she struggled up to her room, flung herself onto her bed and sobbed. He had taken the wind right out of her sails. She was supposed to be the one who won the battle when she accused him of being the worst dad in the world. She had wanted him to feel the full force of her anger. She had been thinking of leaving of her own free will.

Now it had happened, though, it was more than she could bear. Had she been really serious about going?

Well, even if he hadn't actually meant to throw her out, she would show him. She would leave anyway. That would make him feel bad … guilty even. Good. She hoped he would suffer as much as *she* was suffering.

She jumped up and paced the floor, but it didn't make her feel any better. She looked round her room. It had been her own space for as long as she could remember. But now the hard, cold fact kept coming back to her. She was going to have to leave.

It was just getting light when Vicky lay down on her bed again. She tossed and turned and, when at last she slept, she had weird and frightening dreams. When she woke up several hours later it was broad daylight, but nothing had changed. The truth stared her in the face. Nobody wanted her around.

She listened. All quiet. She glanced at her watch. Eleven o'clock. She crept out onto the landing. Silence. Sniffing back the tears, a mixture of anger and regret, she went downstairs, but it was as she suspected. There was no one in the house. She had been abandoned. Her mum and dad must be at work. Katie would be at nursery. Then she remembered that Matt had one of his important exams today. He must be in the middle of it by now.

'I'll be gone before any of them get home,' she said out loud. 'No goodbyes. I'll just vanish from their lives.'

She couldn't stop the tears or the tightness in her chest as she returned to her room and started collecting things together. But when she saw the gigantic pile of stuff on her bed she gasped.

'I can't take all this,' she muttered.

She shoved everything back into her drawers.

'I'll just take what I really *need*,' she said. 'Think straight, Vick. Underwear, socks, jeans, T-shirts.' She found these. 'One skirt, sweaters, cagoul, scarf – though I hope I won't need them this time of year – gloves, woolly hat! Trainers, spares. Sleeping bag and foam roll. How am I going to carry all this? I'll have to borrow Matt's rucksack. Make-up, hair stuff, toiletries, towel. Phone – not that anyone will care whether I ring them or not. I'll take it though. Keep it turned off. Just have it for emergencies. Purse, money. Last, but not least, Bruno.' She gave him a quick hug. 'I can't leave you behind.'

She hurried into Matt's room and found his rucksack. He would be narked when he found it was gone, but she would let him have it back one day. She scribbled him a note.

Matt, I'm sure your life will be much more peaceful when I've gone. I've borrowed your rucksack. I'll let you have it back when I can afford to buy one of my own. Vicky.

It took her the best part of an hour to pack everything and cram her sleeping bag into its sack. Taking a last look around her room, she pulled on her blue hoodie, shoved Bruno in the top of the rucksack and staggered down the stairs. She grabbed a few things from the fridge, then, shouldering the heavy rucksack, she headed for the front door.

She thought about stopping at Uncle Tom's, but remembered he would be at work. Anyway, he'd do his best to try and stop her. She even thought about calling at Lizzie's, but what would be the point? They'd grown miles apart lately.

'Well, at least I've got quite a bit of money,' she said, to cheer herself up as she trudged along the road. 'It'll tide me over until I get a job.'

She made for the railway station.

'London, please,' she said at the ticket office.

'Return?'

'No, single,' she said. That was very hard to say. It made everything sound so final. One way ticket. No return.

She bit her lip and refused to let herself cry. No, she had to be hard from now on. Hard and canny. There would be plenty of people out there ready to take advantage of her. She was not that naïve.

She found an almost empty carriage, sat with her back to everyone and counted her money. Almost £50 left after buying the ticket. Not a lot, but enough. When she had her job and a little bed-sitter, everything would be fine.

At last, the train rattled into the terminus and juddered to a halt. People poured onto the platform like so many zombies, each knowing exactly where they were going, or so it seemed to Vicky, who stood staring along the platform, totally confused. She had been to London several times before, but she had never been here alone.

'All right, love?' asked a railway worker. 'You look lost.'

'Oh, no,' said Vicky quickly, swallowing the lump in her throat. 'I'm fine.'

She marched along the platform as briskly as the weight of her rucksack would allow and pushed her ticket into the slot at the barrier. Ahead of her was a small café where she ordered a cup of tea and sat down to think.

London, the big smoke, large, busy ... anonymous. That was what she wanted to be – anonymous. Nobody was going to find her in such a big place amongst so many millions of people.

The first thing she would do was find a job. She visualised herself as a top model, or the manager of a fashion shop, or a cosmetics consultant. Then she came down to Earth. It would have to be shop assistant or waitressing or even cleaning or washing up, just to begin. The others would come later.

She watched the staff in the coffee shop. Something like this would be good, but not here in this station. That way she would easily be traced. She would probably find herself serving her next door neighbours, or even her friends.

Time to move on. She finished her tea and hoisted the rucksack onto her back. It felt heavier than before. Perhaps she shouldn't have packed so much, but she couldn't imagine what she could have left out. As she walked along the streets she searched for signs advertising for staff, but there were none. She went into several cafes and shops and asked, but no one had any vacancies.

London didn't seem to be the exciting place she remembered from her previous visits. It was very different from those times she had come here with the family. All the famous buildings were magic then and the shows were dazzling and loud and fantastic. Even the museums were full of amazing stuff. Now, everything looked dirty and shoddy. Everywhere was buzzing with crowds of faceless people. Nobody had time to stop and smile.

I wonder what they're doing at home, now they've realised I've gone.

She peered into shops and boutiques where groups of girls were giggling, trying everything on, posing then laughing.

Just like I used to be with Lizzie and the others. I wish they could be with me now.

The evening rush hour and a grumbling stomach told her it was time to eat, but more urgently she realised she had to find somewhere to sleep. She began asking around, but soon realised that it was going to be no easier than finding a job. She stood at the entrance to a tube station. It should be quite easy to get to the main line station from there.

I could go home. I've got enough money for the fare. I could say I was only having them on. Just wanted to give them a bit of a shock.

She shook herself. What was she thinking of?

Grovel to dad? Say I won't be a naughty girl? Promise to do as I'm told? Not on your life! No.. I won't go back, not even if he gets down on his knees and begs me.

A new life was what she wanted, somewhere where she would be valued, where she wasn't compared with a brainbox brother or a sickly-sweet sister, somewhere that allowed her to enjoy herself instead of always having to tell lies, or do things behind people's backs, or sneak in and out, or just stay at home and be miserable.

No! She was determined to stick to her decision. She was staying.

Chapter
SIX

Rush hour was over. It was beginning to get dark. Slowly the streets were becoming deserted and a fear crept over Vicky. Being out alone at night near home was frightening enough, but the city was much worse. It was so big and impersonal and full of unknown dangers.

Suppose I can't find anywhere to sleep.

The bright lights of a burger bar beckoned to her. Nervously, she pushed open the heavy glass door and approached the counter. Soon she was wolfing the cheapest burger she could buy. As she ate, she looked around her. There were a few couples, an older man and several young people sitting on their own, but none of them made eye contact. Nobody seemed the least bit interested in her.

She felt better with a full stomach, but the frightening fact still remained. She had nowhere to sleep.

'On your own?'

Vicky snapped out of her day-dreams. The older man had joined her at her table. Red lights flashed warnings in her brain.

'Oh, no,' she lied, turning her back on him. 'I'm meeting a friend.'

'Suit yourself,' said the man, slinking away.

Vicky gripped the table firmly to stop herself from shaking. He might have been innocent, but how could she be sure? She didn't need that kind of thing to rattle her. Outside the burger bar Vicky was confronted again. This time, the man was in uniform. The Salvation Army.

'Saw you in there,' he said. 'Saw that man talking to you. Are you all right?'

'Yes, thanks,' said Vicky, giving nothing away. How did she know this man was really a member of the Sally Army? He could be a con man or a thief – or worse.

A woman in the same uniform came up to them. She looked kind and homely, rather like Grandma. Her smile was warm and friendly.

'There's our soup kitchen just down the road, dear,' she said. 'And we could see if there's room in the hostel tonight, if that's what you need.'

Vicky relaxed her guard. Not completely. Just enough to nod her head and follow the woman to the corner of the next street.

'Here we are, dear,' said the woman when they stopped at a large van. 'Mary will look after you, won't you, Mary?'

Mary, another woman in uniform, stood beside an enormous vat of soup. She smiled, too.

'Of course I will, Gladys,' she said.

'Wait here,' said Gladys, 'and I'll check the hostel.'

Vicky stood by the van and held the mug of soup in both hands. She slowly sipped it. It was warm and comforting, and very tasty.

'Homeless?' Mary asked.

Vicky shrugged her shoulders. She would keep her affairs to herself.

'Family row?'

Vicky glanced up at her. How did she know?

'Happens all the time,' said Mary. 'Every night we get youngsters turn up here. Think London is just the place to escape to. Had a row with their parents ... Run away or thrown out?'

'Thrown out,' said Vicky. 'No, left of my own accord.'

'Can't go crawling home with your tail between your legs, can you, dear?'

Vicky shook her head. It was uncanny how the woman seemed to understand.

Gladys came scurrying back out of the darkness.

'Good news,' she said. 'There's room in the hostel.'

Vicky felt the tension in her body relax. At least she would have a roof over her head. She followed Gladys along more dark lonely streets until they reached a tall, dingy building.

'This is it,' said Gladys.

'Thanks,' Vicky said, as they parted at the door.

'My pleasure. Goodbye, dear. If you need us again, you know where to find us. We're here every night.'

Vicky was taken inside and shown up to the bedroom. There were several beds in the room, all occupied except one. Some women were asleep. Others stared unsmiling at her over the grey blankets that covered them.

'Thanks,' Vicky said to the warden, her heart sinking to her feet. What a contrast to her lovely room at home! This room was stark and clinical. *Still, beggars can't be choosers*, she thought, suddenly understanding the meaning of the phrase for the first time.

She carried her rucksack into the bathroom and used the toilet and the shower, not taking her eyes off her belongings for a second. Gladys had warned her on the way there.

'I'm not suggesting that everyone you'll meet is a thief,' she had said, 'but remember, these people have nothing. Just don't give any of them a chance.'

Vicky eyed the occupants of the room suspiciously when she returned to the bedroom then, after tucking her valuables under her pillow and clutching Bruno, she got into bed. Several women had watched her every move.

'First night, is it?' one asked.

Vicky didn't reply. Was it that obvious? Feeling desperately sorry for herself, she buried her head in her pillow and sobbed. After a while, she dried her eyes and tried to snuggle down on the hard bed.

'You'll get used to it,' said another woman.

'It's all right this time of year,' said the first one. 'But you wait till the winter. It's hell.'

With those comforting words echoing round her brain, Vicky fell into a light sleep. She dreamed of little girls with blond curls and frilly pink dresses, each of them sticking their tongues out and laughing. They all looked remarkably like Katie.

Suddenly, she woke up, the vision of her little sister instantly gone from her mind. Someone was beside her bed, delving in her rucksack. Vicky sat up and screamed. The woman dashed back to her own bed.

'Leave my things alone!' shouted Vicky, more startled than angry.

No one moved or made a sound.

She checked under her pillow and in her rucksack. Nothing was missing. She had woken in time.

Lying down again, she thought of her dream. She pictured Katie, glad that her troublesome big sister had gone. She wondered what things were like at home. Everybody would be pleased that she had left them in peace. Katie would enjoy demanding even more of everyone's attention. Matt would be glad he could work for his exams undisturbed. Mum would be more relaxed. And Dad – well, he would be glowing with self-satisfaction, now he had got rid of the bane of his life.

Or would they?

Hoping that the other occupants of the room wouldn't try anything a second time, Vicky clutched the rucksack with one hand and hugged Bruno to her chest with the other, and drifted off to sleep.

Chapter SEVEN

When Vicky woke, she found she was still clutching the rucksack and Bruno. She felt under her pillow. Nothing missing. It was light, but the streets were quite quiet. The other women were still asleep.

I wonder what they're doing at home. Even if they're glad, I bet they're shocked. I bet they didn't think I'd have the guts to go!

She quietly climbed out of bed and scrounged in her rucksack for her sponge bag and hair brush. It would be best if she could make herself as respectable as possible if she was going to get a decent job.

'Today's got to be better than yesterday,' she

whispered to Bruno, as she tucked him into a side pocket of the rucksack. 'As soon as I get a job, I'll find a place of my own. Get myself on my feet.'

She crept towards the bathroom, trying not to wake the others, but she bumped the rucksack into the foot of one of the beds.

'What's ya name?'

Vicky spun round. The woman who had tried to steal from her was watching her from under her blanket. She had slate-grey eyes that stared, cold and hard. The nerve!

'That's my business,' said Vicky.

She had been thinking about this. She wasn't going to give anything away about herself. Not to anybody. That way, if they came looking for her she wouldn't be traced. She would have to change her name. To what?

Another woman sat up and rubbed her eyes.

'G'day,' she said, stretching. 'I slept terrible last night. Lumpy bed, scratchy blanket. What kind of a doss house do they call this? Your country's a dump, no mistake. I can't wait to get back to Oz.'

Vicky washed and made up her face as she thought about what the woman had said. Oz. *I like*

*it. Easy. Yes, a good name. Exit Vicky. From now on,
I'm Oz.*

As soon as Oz had eaten breakfast, she left the hostel.

One thing was definite, she thought, as she
trudged along the dusty streets. That place was all
right for her first night and it was kind of Gladys to
find it for her, but she wouldn't stay there again.

But the day was as frustrating as the one before.
She went into endless shops, restaurants, cafes and
offices, but nobody had a job to offer her, not even
cleaning or washing up. Wherever she went,
everyone seemed to be rushing about, minding their
own business. None of them had a smile for her. No
one spoke to her. She felt incredibly lonely.

By nightfall she had succeeded in doing nothing
except spend some of her precious money on fast food
and drinks. Feeling very depressed, she took back the
promise she had made to herself that morning and
found her way back to the hostel. But the warden
shook her head.

'Sorry, dear,' she said. 'We're overcrowded as it is.
Try the one down the road.'

Oz was sent from hostel to hostel, but they were all full to bursting. She found the kind women from the Salvation Army, but although they gave her some soup and a friendly smile, they knew of nowhere else for her to sleep.

'I hope you don't mind my suggesting this,' Mary said as Oz sipped her soup. 'But have you thought about going home?'

She had. It had been on her mind all day. She had often been tempted to switch on her mobile and phone. It would be the easiest thing in the world to ring home. Would her dad come and fetch her? She wasn't sure if he would. Then each time she had seen the familiar logo above a tube station she was tempted to make that journey, but each time she had refused to give in.

She nodded. 'I can't,' she said. 'They'll all be celebrating.'

'Surely not.'

'My brother's doing his A levels. He'll do much better with me out of the way. And my little sister will think it's the best thing that's ever happened to her.'

'What about your parents? Have you thought how concerned they must be?'

Oz shrugged her shoulders. 'I don't know,' she said. 'One minute they reckoned they were worried about me and the next they were being mean and unreasonable.'

'Aren't you missing them?'

Oz shook her head. She wasn't going to admit that to anyone, especially to a stranger.

'Well dear, don't wait too long before you go back.'

Oz suddenly felt annoyed with Mary. She had been a good listener, but she had no right to tell Oz what to do. *She* didn't know what the rest of the family was like.

Oz put her mug of unfinished soup down and walked sadly away. As she did so, the urgency of her situation struck her. She had to find somewhere to rest for the night.

First, she tried the Underground. She crept into one of the tunnels and began to lay out her foam bed roll, but she was soon moved on from there. She tried a shop doorway, but the same thing happened. She tried not to let it worry her. It wouldn't matter. It was a fine night. She would have to sleep in the open air. Anywhere. She just needed to rest.

The last time she had slept in the open air was at

school camp, but this was nothing like that. Now there was no tent over her head. There were no friends to laugh and gossip with and no teacher to tell them all to be quiet.

She eventually chose a spot off the main road. It was a quiet area under some trees, but there were quite a few people about. She didn't want to be too far away from help if she needed it. She snuggled down inside her sleeping bag, wide-eyed and frightened. But how was she going to sleep in such an exposed place? Anyone could come along in the middle of the night and attack her or rob her. She would have to stay awake. She felt too tense to sleep anyway.

For a long time, she watched people go by. Some were alone. Some were in groups or in pairs, men and women, old and young, smart or scruffy. Some looked all right, but others looked rough and threatening.

Many people ignored her or pretended they hadn't seen her. A few people looked at her and one or two threw a coin onto her bag. Then a young man stepped right over her and another gave her a kick in the ribs. Each time anyone came towards her, she tensed up, ready to react if they came too near.

One of her worst moments came when an ugly old man came and stood by her. Her body was rigid with fear as he bent over and peered short-sightedly at her face.

'Scum!' he hissed, pointing a grubby finger at her.

Suddenly, he spat. Oz didn't have time to dodge away and his stinking spittle landed dangerously close to her face. She felt sick with fear and disgust, but she dare not speak.

'Scum!' he hissed again, then he ambled unsteadily away.

It took several minutes for her heart to slow down. She hoped every night would not be like this. She would never get any sleep.

But slowly the streets became quiet and, eventually, Oz slept.

The next morning, she felt terrible when she woke. Her head throbbed and her eyes were smarting. She felt grimy and miserable.

'What am I doing?' she muttered to herself as she rolled up her bedding. 'Perhaps I should go home today.'

But how could she face everyone now? She would give it a few more days. Maybe things would improve.

But that day and the next rolled into one. Each day was the same. Nobody needed staff, nobody had a room cheap enough for her to afford, and the money in her purse was slowly being eaten away.

A week went by. The trouble was, she realised, she was getting into a downward spiral. The longer she was living on the streets, the scruffier she became. The scruffier she looked, the less chance she stood in getting a job. If she had no job, she wouldn't be able to afford a room. And if the money ran out, what then?

She felt she would be able to cope better if it weren't for all the other people living on the streets. There were so many of them, always competing for the good places to sleep and the beds in the hostels. But none of them seemed interested in making friends with Oz. She missed having a laugh with Lizzie and the others. She wondered if they missed her, whether they thought she was an idiot, whether any of them cared about what happened to her.

Normally, she would have phoned Lizzie by now and confided in her. Lizzie would have told her to stop being a loser. But since that row at the disco things hadn't been the same. She couldn't face it.

Lizzie might laugh or cut her off. That would be worse than not speaking to her at all. No. It was best not to phone.

At least the charities were always dishing out soup or sandwiches. And there were clothes hand outs. Not the fashion she was used to, but useful.

Useful? She couldn't believe that she was thinking like this! And she felt so dirty. No hot showers on tap, like she'd had at home. It was a different world to the one she had grown up in.

Gradually, she was learning by experience. You had to be careful who you spoke to. Some people seemed nice enough one moment, then turned against you the next. Trust nobody! But the loneliness was the worst. That just wouldn't go away.

'There must be someone like me,' she whispered to Bruno one night. 'Someone I can talk to.'

But if there was, she never met her or him. Every day she was tempted to give in, to phone or to go home and ask everyone to forgive her. And every day she fought against it. She would have to grit her teeth and carry on.

'You got yourself into this, Vicky, Oz, whoever you are,' she told herself. 'So it's down to you. You're on your own!'

Chapter
EIGHT

Gradually, Oz got used to her new life. She often thought about her family, but she always managed to stop herself phoning home.

I won't forgive Dad. And I won't go crawling back.

But one day she was sitting on a low wall with Bruno in her arms. She was holding out her hand in case anyone was feeling generous that morning. All her money had gone.

'Here,' said an attractive girl who stopped beside her. 'Take these.' She placed a few coins in Oz's hand. 'Make a phone call. Let them know you're still alive.'

Oz stared at her. *I bet she's only a few years older than me. Why should she care?*

'I was the same as you a few months ago,' said the girl. 'It only needed me to make one phone call. Went back home the next day. The best thing I ever did.'

Oz watched her back as she walked away. Was she telling the truth? Had she been homeless? Or was she just some busy-body, thinking she knew all about it, but really knowing nothing?

Oz looked at the coins in her hand. They would buy a bun or a drink, or go towards a burger. She didn't need the money for a phone call – she had her mobile, after all – but maybe the girl was right. What harm would phoning do?

Before she could change her mind, she delved into the rucksack and pulled out her phone. With shaking fingers, she switched it on. Good! The battery hadn't gone flat. She dialled the number. It was answered immediately. She was too stunned to speak at first.

'Hello? Hello?' It was Great Aunt Sheila's sharp voice. 'Who is it?'

'Hello.' Oz spoke very quietly.

'Victoria! Is that you?'

'Yes.'

'Well, I hope you're satisfied.'

'What d'you mean?'

'You've caused absolute mayhem here,' Aunt Sheila ranted. 'Your poor parents, to have an ungrateful daughter like you. Where are you?'

'London.'

'Streets paved with gold, are they?'

Oz hated the sarcastic tone. 'No.'

'They've all been out searching, going frantic. I told them, "She doesn't deserve a moment's thought," – but they won't listen to me.'

'Tell them not to bother,' Oz said angrily, then hung up. She had never really liked her mum's aunt, but that had made her mad. She thrust the mobile back into the rucksack, trying to kid herself that she hadn't been upset by the news that everyone had been searching for her. Perhaps they *did* care.

'I wonder where they've been looking,' she whispered to Bruno.

Sleeping in the open air was bearable on warm clear nights, but one night the rain came. It was sweeping rain that soaked you to the skin and seeped into everything. All night and the following day the rain lashed down and Oz huddled with others under any shelter they could find. That was where she met Paul.

'Been living rough long?' he asked, as they stood close together under a bridge, watching the rain and wondering if it would ever stop.

'A few weeks,' said Oz. 'You?'

'A year or so. I dunno. I lost track.'

'Why don't you go home?'

'Haven't got one. I'm an orphan. Grew up in a children's home. Had to leave when I was sixteen.'

Oz gasped. There she was, moaning about her parents and Paul didn't even have any.

'Sorry. I didn't realise,' she said.

'S'all right,' said Paul. 'I'm used to having nowhere to go now.'

'Have you been in London all the time?'

'I was in Manchester until last month.'

'Why d'you come south?' Oz studied his profile silhouetted against the grey sky. If he had a wash and brush up and a clean set of clothes he'd be quite good looking.

'I dunno,' he said again. 'One place is as good as the next, I reckon, when you've got nothing to do.'

Oz quite liked being close to someone after all this time. Human contact and all that. An old bear is fine for comfort, but not particularly the best company! She pushed herself a few centimetres nearer and felt his arm wrap round her shoulder. It felt good. She smiled up at him. It was great to smile, once in a while.

'Paul,' he said.

'Oz.'

He's obviously feeling the same as me, she thought. Needs someone.

The rain stopped. Oz shouldered her rucksack and stepped out into the glistening street.

'Mind if I tag along?' he said.

'Please yourself,' she said, not letting him see her delight.

They didn't talk much, but it was lovely to walk side by side as if they were friends. Two waifs brought together by a rain storm, which started again with a vengeance. They scuttled into a shop doorway.

'You hungry?' Paul asked.

Oz nodded. 'But I'm skint.'

'On me,' he said. From his pocket he produced a handful of coins.

'Magic,' she said. 'You're rich. How come?'

'Busking,' he said.

'What with?'

'Paper and comb.'

Oz giggled. Paper and comb!

'Mock not,' said Paul. 'If you want something to eat, that is!'

There was a special offer on in the burger bar and Oz feasted on burger and a milkshake and felt bloated afterwards. When they came out it had stopped raining.

'Now to earn tomorrow's grub,' said Paul, taking a filthy comb and some tissue paper out of his pocket.

He found a corner spot on the pavement and began to hum through the comb. Once Oz had recovered from her embarrassment, she began to listen. He was quite talented. She watched people throwing their small change into Paul's hat on the ground. If only she could do something like that.

'How much we got?' Paul asked after about half an hour.

'A few quid, I should think,' said Oz.

Paul picked up his hat and pocketed the coins. The rain, which had held off for Paul's performance, now teemed down yet again.

'It's set in for the night,' he said. 'Come on. Let's find a pitch.'

The dry spots had all been taken. Oz began to feel depression pulling her down as they splashed from puddle to puddle for what seemed an age. Night was falling early, but there seemed to be nowhere for them to go.

I must be mad! I'm cold and wet and tired. No place to sleep. I bet they're all cosy and snug at home. I could so easily phone again.

But Paul began beckoning.

'It's all right. I know somewhere,' he said. 'Found it by accident the other night. Come on.'

Oz followed him along the darkening streets until they turned into a blind alley behind a restaurant. Oz hung back. Should she go any further with him? Who was he? She had only met him a few hours before. Should she trust him?

Paul smiled. It was such a boyish, friendly smile. What harm could he do her?

'Come on,' said Paul, pushing open a door that creaked on its hinges. 'It's OK.'

So, with a glance over her shoulder, Oz entered the building. In the darkness she sensed the vastness of the place. Their footsteps echoed as they trod across the stone floor. She shuddered and stepped nearer to Paul.

'Where are we?'

'You're shaking,' he said, taking hold of her hand. 'I told you, it's OK. It's only an empty warehouse. No one uses it. No one will know.'

'I'm so cold.'

She didn't need to tell Paul how she felt. Her eyes filled with tears and she slumped down onto the ground and sobbed.

'Don't,' he said, crouching beside her, stroking her sodden hair.

She leaned towards him and let him take her in his arms.

'I'm so miserable,' she cried into his chest. 'I didn't fit in at home. I came away because I couldn't stand it any longer, but what am I going to do?'

'First, you need to get dry,' said Paul. 'We both do.'

Gradually Oz's eyes got used to the dark. Then Paul struck a match and lit a candle that Oz presumed he must have left there before. She could see other signs of habitation, too. Some old blankets on the ground with a poly bag beside them.

'Come and sit on these,' he said. 'They're not very clean, but they're dry.'

Oz allowed Paul to help her take off her sodden shoes and socks and her jeans. Her teeth chattered noisily as her cagoul and sweater joined the soggy pile on the floor. She sat wrapped in a blanket as Paul's clothes made a pile next to hers and then he snuggled beside her under his blanket. From the carrier bag, he produced two cans of cola.

'Cheers!' he said as he raised his can.

Oz couldn't help smiling. He was doing his best to cheer her up. He was kind and friendly. The first really nice person she had met in ages.

'Better?' he asked when they had both emptied their cans.

Oz nodded. The cola had tasted heavenly. 'Thanks,' she said, with a smile.

Suddenly, Paul reached out and pulled her towards him. Was he going to kiss her?

'No,' she said, pushing him away.

She wasn't into kissing total strangers! Especially here, in this dark sinister place. He had said that no one used the warehouse. No one would know they were there! It struck her like a blow to the stomach.

She could be in terrible danger!

She scrambled to her feet and hurried to her rucksack.

'What's up?' he asked.

'I've got to go,' she said, finding a dry set of clothes.

'Where?'

'Anywhere.'

'At this time of night? Don't be an idiot. Stay.'

As she pulled on the clothes, she found she was shaking again, not with cold, but with fear.

What a fool I am. Coming to this isolated place. Exposing myself to danger. I should have listened to myself earlier.

'Don't go.' Paul was standing up and coming towards her.

She backed off. 'Stay away from me!'

He stopped and put his hands up in front of him. 'No sweat,' he said.

He might be harmless, but she couldn't risk it. What was she doing here anyway?

Her mind was made up. She had stuck at this miserable life long enough. She was going to have to swallow her pride and ring them.

Stuffing her sodden clothes into the poly bag and fighting the choking tears that began to overwhelm her, she hoisted the rucksack onto her back and stumbled from the warehouse.

Chapter
NINE

It was still raining. Blindly, Oz roamed the streets, unable to rest. She looked at her watch. It was 3 a.m. She couldn't phone home now, in the middle of the night. Maybe in the morning.

Suddenly, a menacing figure leapt out of the darkness. Oz squinted against the bright torch beam that was directed straight into her face. All she could see was a dark anorak with the hood pulled up, shading all but a pair of dark, evil eyes.

'Who's that?' she asked, her voice quaking.

'Nobody,' snapped a rough female voice.

'What do you want?'

Oz inhaled sharply as the torch beam flickered on something in the girl's other hand. Was it a knife?

'Money.'

'I'm broke,' said Oz, hoping the girl would believe her.

'What have you got then?'

The girl flashed the torch beam onto Oz's watch. 'That.' She pointed the knife. 'Quick!'

Oz was so terrified she would have given the girl everything. She fumbled with the watch strap in her haste to undo it then she almost dropped it as she held it out to the girl, who snatched it, clicked off the torch and disappeared into the darkness.

Oz sat down on a low wall to recover. She could feel her pulse racing and her breathing was tight and shallow. She was too stunned to cry.

What a night! Could it get any worse?

As her heartbeat slowed and her breathing became more normal, she stood up. Although her legs felt as weak as a sponge, she hurried towards the busier streets. She would stay in the light from the shops and restaurants from now on. Beginning to feel dizzy as dawn broke, she slumped down exhausted in the doorway of a restaurant. Please God they wouldn't be opening until lunch time. Might give her a chance to sleep.

When she woke, a girl was sitting beside her. Oz's heart thumped again. She clasped her rucksack to her and stared at the girl suspiciously. Was this the girl who had just robbed her?

'What d'you want?' she demanded roughly.

'Just sheltering,' said the girl. 'Like you.'

Oz studied the girl's face. It was thin and pale and she didn't look at all well. She had a sharp pointed nose and the biggest, darkest rings around her grey eyes. But they weren't those evil eyes of the thief. And she wasn't wearing an anorak.

'Got any food?' asked the girl. 'I'm starving.'

'Not a crumb,' said Oz.

She sat up and looked around. The streets were quiet. She wondered what the time was and how long she had slept. The girl reached out and touched Oz on the arm. Oz flinched and drew back.

'What's up with you?' asked the girl.

Oz glanced at her. She looked upset by Oz's reaction.

'I had a bad experience last night, that's all.'

'Bad experience? What sort?'

Oz was reluctant to confide in this girl who had appeared out of the blue grey morning mist. She had already been taken in by someone seeming sympathetic, but she needed to talk. Should she trust this girl?

'I'm Jo,' said the girl.

'Oz.'

'I'm a good listener,' said Jo. 'Fire away.'

Oz hesitated for a moment longer, then made up her mind and began a detailed account of the previous evening's experiences. Jo listened patiently, nodding every now and then, her face drained of all colour. Oz felt so much better for getting it off her chest.

Jo said nothing. She sat staring into space for so long that Oz became concerned.

'Have I said something wrong?' she asked.

Jo blinked and shook herself.

'No,' she said. 'It's nothing.'

Oz was curious. Why did she suddenly feel sorry for this girl?

'I'm a good listener, too,' she said. 'If you want to tell me.'

'My mum and dad got divorced. I wanted to go with Dad, but for some reason Mum got custody. To cut a long story, Mum married again.'

Oz could see how difficult it had become for Jo to go on. She was clenching her arms tightly round her knees.

'My step-father was a foul pig. I won't go into details … I can't bear to talk about it … In the end I couldn't stand living there with them any longer. So I've run away. There's no way they'll come looking for me. He's glad to be rid of me and Mum's so besotted with him she won't even notice. She had turned against me. Said I was trying to wreck her marriage.'

Jo burst into tears. Oz reached out and held her hand.

'That makes my reason for leaving home so pathetic,' said Oz. 'My dad's hard and strict, but he's not a monster.'

She told Jo all about home.

'Why don't you go back?' asked Jo. 'I bet they're desperately worried.'

'But I don't know if I can face them now.'

'Why don't you ring?'

82

Oz had been waiting for the moment and now it had arrived. She smiled at Jo then she eagerly pulled out her mobile and turned it on.

Blank. She shook it, tapped it and tried again. Zilch!

'Oh sugar!' she cried. 'It would happen now. The battery's flat. I must have left it on.' She had forgotten to bring her charger, but anyway, there was nowhere to plug it in.

'Use a call box then,' said Jo.

'No money. You haven't got any, I suppose?'

'Not a bean. You could reverse the charges.'

Oz shook her head. She couldn't do that. It would look as if she was pleading.

'Oh, well,' she said. 'It was a good idea. Thanks.'

Jo got up. She began packing her things away.

'I'd better be moving on,' she said.

'Where to?'

'Anywhere,' said Jo.

The grey sky had cleared, but a chilly wind whistled along the street. People rushed by as Oz forced her sleeping bag into the rucksack. Jo was already walking away.

'Wait,' called Oz. 'Can I come with you?'

'Why not?' said Jo.

Oz and Jo trudged together for hours, chatting and getting to know each other. Oz liked her new friend. She found they had lot of things in common.

Later that day they came to a huge railway bridge over the River Thames, with arches that continued all the way to a main line station. There, among several other homeless people, they found a dry space to sleep.

'Our patch,' said Jo, cheerfully. 'This will do nicely until we move into the Palace!'

Oz chuckled. It made her feel good. Things were looking up. She would ring home when she had some money, but for now she wasn't so miserable or lonely.

Using the railway arch as their base, the two girls managed to dry out their clothes. For the next few days they stayed in the little area that was their temporary home. They got to know old Jim, their neighbour, and Sue, a strange, middle-aged woman, and several other people.

Oz and Jo made an agreement. One of them would always guard their belongings while the other went out for food or drink from one of the charities, or to use the public toilet nearby. These people all seemed honest enough, but how could they be sure? The girls trusted each other, but agreed to trust nobody else.

Oz was happy to chat away with Jo. It was almost like being with Lizzie. But she wished they could buy their food instead of having to rely on hand-outs all the time.

'We should try busking,' she said one evening. 'That boy, Paul, that I told you about. He earned loads of money with a comb and paper.'

'But how can we?' asked Jo. 'I can't sing or dance or play comb and paper.'

'Nor can I,' Oz sighed.

'Anyway, I'd feel too embarrassed.'

Oz had to admit she would, too.

'But I need to get money from somewhere,' she said. 'I really want to phone home soon.'

Chapter
TEN

The next morning, Oz couldn't believe her luck. She was returning to the arches, carrying a food hand-out from the charity CRISIS, when she found a 50p coin in a crevice at the side of the path. She picked it up and hurried back to show Jo.

'I'll be able to ring home this evening,' said Oz, with a bright look on her face.

'You won't get very long on the phone with that!' said Jo. 'But it's better than nothing.'

'If only I could earn some money,' sighed Oz. 'I could phone for as long as I liked.'

'Or you could go home,' said Jo.

There was a loud cough from old Jim, a few metres along the arch.

'Don't mind my eavesdropping,' he said. 'But are you wanting to earn money?'

The girls both nodded.

'Well,' said Jim. 'I might be able to help you there.'

'How?' asked Jo.

'Some friends of mine are heading out of town,' said Jim. 'They say there's plenty of work. Strawberry picking.'

Oz leapt up, excited. She looked at Jo. 'Well?' she said.

'I'm on,' said Jo, with a big grin.

'So am I,' said Oz, bending to give her friend a hug. Then she turned to their neighbour. 'All right, Jim. When do we start?'

'Always moving about the country, my friends are,' said Jim. 'And they say they're leaving town this afternoon.'

'But will they want us to go with them?' asked Jo.

'They need a couple more people, they told me last night. There's always millions of strawberries to be picked at this time of year. You get so much a basket.'

'Great!' said Oz, as she and Jo began to pack up their things. 'Are you coming, too?'

'No, it's back-breaking work,' said Jim. 'I'm much too old. I'll stay here and keep your pitch warm.'

Oz smiled at him. He had been a good neighbour, but she didn't intend coming back, warm pitch or not!

'Thanks,' she said.

'Where can we meet your friends?' asked Jo.

'At the Elephant and Castle,' said Jim. 'It's a couple of miles from here. I'll take you, if you like.'

'Oh, Jim,' said Oz, beaming at him. 'You're fantastic!'

'Fantastic!' echoed Jim with wide grin that exposed uneven, blackened teeth. 'I've been called lots of things in my time, but that's the first time I've been called that!'

They were ready. Oz heaved her rucksack onto her back and they followed Jim out into the street. It was a lovely day, just right for travelling to the country. With a bit of luck, she would soon be earning good money.

They found Jim's friends on a piece of waste land off a side street at the back of a large pub. There were two vans and two battered old caravans, a group of men and women and three little children. Oz held back when she saw them. These people wouldn't want intruders getting in their way.

The smallest child ran towards them.

'Hey, Jim!' she yelled.

'Hey, Tinkerbell,' said Jim, patting the little girl on the head.

'Who are you?' asked the child, staring at the girls.

A woman hurried over to them.

'Don't mind our Tinkerbell,' she said. 'Come and join us. Any friend of Jim's is a friend of ours.'

Oz felt her tensed up shoulders relax. The woman had such a welcoming smile on her chubby brown face. No-one could be nervous with her for long.

'I'm Hazel,' said the woman. She pointed at the other people as they walked over. 'That skinny one here's my man. He's Rowan. Them other three's Holly and Dave and Mungo. The kids are all mine. That's Silvan and Flora and Tinkerbell.'

'Oz and Jo,' said Jim, pointing to the girls in turn.

'The more, the merrier,' said Rowan, walking towards them.

'We spend most of our lives on the road,' said Hazel. 'Here one day, gone tomorrow – that's us.'

'We move to where the work is,' said Rowan.

The children began chasing each other round the vans, shouting and laughing. Oz smiled at them. She hadn't realised how much she missed having a little one around.

'Can I sit by you?' asked Flora, coming back to Oz and taking her hand.

'OK,' said Oz with a smile, as they all crammed into the vans.

On her other side, Oz found herself crushed against a tall young lad called Dave, and it wasn't long before she was bowled over by his crazy sense of humour.

'He's gorgeous,' she whispered to Bruno as she made sure he was tucked safely in the pocket of the rucksack. 'Those deep brown eyes. I could fall for him!'

Dave teased the children and kept everyone amused with his corny jokes.

'How do you stop a skunk smelling?'

'I don't know.'

'Hold its nose!'

Everyone laughed.

'What do you get if you cross an elephant with a garden hose?'

'Give up.'

'A jumbo jet!'

'You sound like a walking Christmas cracker!' said Mungo, who was driving.

But it made the uncomfortable ride out of London much easier. The journey lasted for two or three hours, but with everyone in such a cheerful mood the time passed quickly. And what amazed Oz more than anything else, the children behaved perfectly, joining in the conversation like mini adults.

They were well out of London when Oz became aware of Mungo's eyes on her in the driving mirror. She looked away embarrassed, but a little later, the same thing happened again.

'Sorry,' said Mungo. 'I don't mean to stare, but I'm trying for the life of me to work out where I've seen you before.'

'Me?' said Oz, amazed.

'Yeah. You look familiar for some reason.'

After a few more miles, Mungo suddenly drove into a lay-by at the side of the road, stopped the van, switched off the engine and turned round to look at Oz.

'I've cracked it!' he said, grinning.

He leaned across and reached inside a bag on the floor of the van and pulled out a magazine.

'*The Big Issue*,' he said, holding it up. 'A great mag! Get it every week when I can. I bought this one yesterday from a homeless bloke.'

He thumbed through the pages.

'Ah! Yes, I was right! Here it is!'

He passed the magazine to Oz. The two girls peered at the page. Oz gasped. There were four photos smiling back out of the magazine. One of them was her!

'*Missing!*' was the headline. '*Can you help?*'

Her real name was underneath the photo, then there was a paragraph about her and how much her family wanted her back. Oz could hardly breathe. She was totally shocked at seeing herself, but even more stunned that her parents had gone to the trouble of putting the appeal in.

They must want me home!

'Wow!' said Jo. 'Your name's Vicky?'

'Not any more. I changed it so I couldn't be found.'

'But we've found you!' said Mungo with a grin as he started the engine. 'Why don't you ring them?'

'I did,' said Oz very quietly. 'Just before I met Jo. But … it didn't go too well.' She didn't need to mention Aunt Sheila. 'But at least they know I'm still alive.'

'You've gone really pale,' said Jo. 'You all right?'

'Just about,' said Oz. But it took her quite a while to get over seeing herself in *The Big Issue*.

'You need to try phoning again,' said Mungo as they set off. 'You might get on better next time.'

Oz nodded. She would, when she got the chance.

Fifteen minutes later, Mungo turned off the main road and drove along a very rough track. They had to hang onto each other as the van lurched from side to side.

'Perfect way to get to know you,' said Dave as he clutched Oz.

Oz couldn't help laughing. She had to agree.

Jo was sitting opposite them. 'This must be the farm,' she said.

'Right first time,' said Mungo. 'OK, one and all. We've arrived.'

Chapter
ELEVEN

The van stopped and the back doors were flung open. Oz crouched inside the van and looked around outside. It was beautiful; rolling hills in one direction, an old farm in the other and a clear blue sky above. Beside the farm buildings, she could see a group of ramshackle huts.

They clambered down onto the hard mud track. The farmer was waiting for them, with his arms folded firmly across his chest and a sour expression on his face.

'Right,' he said. 'This is Beechings Farm. My name's Barnes.'

Oz and Jo glanced at each other and frowned.

'Not very friendly,' whispered Oz.

'Oh, he's all right,' whispered Dave. 'His bark's worse than his bite. Some of us have been here before.'

'Now, a few house rules, before we start,' said the farmer. 'One, you keep the place tidy. Two, you keep quiet after ten at night. Three, you work hard. And four, if you do all that, I'll be paying you. Agreed?'

'Agreed!' said Oz with the others.

It was all new and exciting. Much better than living hand to mouth in the dirty, dangerous streets of the city. She couldn't wait to start.

'Those who won't be sleeping in the caravans,' continued Barnes, pointing, 'can doss down in the huts.'

'They look a bit rickety,' Jo whispered in Oz's ear. 'They probably don't keep the rain out.'

'Well,' whispered Oz. 'The weather's dry for the moment and a hut *is* better than a London street any day.'

Oz smiled at Dave and he pulled a grotesque face in return. Both the girls laughed. Dave was a real clown.

'There's a toilet and shower at the back of the barn,' said the farmer. 'You can have half an hour to get sorted out then come to the farmhouse for some grub. Then, as it's a fine evening, you can get a few hours picking in before dark.'

It was perfect. A roof (even a leaky one) over their heads, an almost en suite bathroom and food laid on.

'I wish we'd heard about this before,' said Jo.

'It wouldn't have done you much good,' said Dave. 'The strawberries would have been sour and green last week.'

'You're right there,' said Mr Barnes. 'And now it's a race against the clock and the weather to get them in. Right, any questions?'

'Is there a phone box near here?' asked Oz.

'Just down the lane,' said the farmer.

'Thanks.'

Very soon, she would let them know where she was. The photo in the magazine had been a huge shock. It was hard to believe, but what was written in the magazine was beginning to sink in and it confirmed what Great Aunt Sheila had said. They were all missing her, even Dad! And she had to admit what she had known all along … she was missing them, too – even Dad!

'I'll race you to our hotel,' shouted Dave, as soon as the farmer had headed back to the farmhouse. 'Come on.'

Dave won the race by miles, so he chose the best corner of the hut, but Oz didn't care. She and Jo found a spot by the window. They were right on the edge of the field, overlooking miles and miles of countryside. They unrolled their bedding. Holly came into the hut carrying a bundle of blankets and two carrier bags.

'Room for a little one?' she asked.

'Of course there is,' said Oz.

She and Jo watched Holly complete her makeshift bed.

'Coming to eat?' said Holly.

'You bet!' said Jo.

'In a bit,' said Oz. 'I'll just go and make a call first. Save some grub for me, will you?'

Clutching the coin she had found tightly in her hand, she ran down the lane. Sure enough, after a couple of minutes, she saw the phone box ahead. Nervously she entered the box and quickly dialled the number before she could change her mind. She hoped she wouldn't get the dreaded Aunt Sheila again.

'Hello?'

'Matt! It's Vicky.' She only just remembered to use her real name. She had got so used to thinking of herself as Oz.

'Vick!' He sounded excited, pleased. 'Are you OK?'

'Yes.' Oz found her throat was dry. She had difficulty speaking. 'Look, we have to be quick. The money will run out. Tell everyone not to worry about me.'

'A bit late for that!' said Matt with a hollow laugh. 'We've all been worried sick.'

Oz swallowed. 'Well, tell them I'm sorry, then.'

'All right.'

'I saw my photo in *The Big Issue*,' she said.

'Great! Did seeing that make you ring?'

'Sort of. I was going to ring anyway, but … How were your exams?'

'I've had worse. I did the last one the day you left.'

'Oh. Good.' That news made Oz feel better. She had been hoping she hadn't ruined his chances of good grades and his place at Uni.

'Katie's missing you.'

'Is she?' Wow! Oz had presumed her little sister would be delighted she had gone.

'She wants you to come home, Vick,' said Matt in a choked sort of voice. 'We all do.'

'Even Dad?'

'Even Dad.'

The pips were going.

'I'll ring again,' Oz shouted over the sound.

'And come home soon,' she heard Matt shout.

Then the phone went dead.

Oz walked back to the farm in a kind of trance. She went to the hut first and sat holding Bruno for a while. Then she got up.

'I'd better go and eat,' she said, as she tucked Bruno well down into her sleeping bag.

She suddenly felt hungrier than she had done for ages.

'It must be the fresh air,' she muttered, as she headed for the farmhouse. She sat down in the seat Jo had saved for her. 'They want me back,' she whispered.

'Go then. Why don't you?'

'I'm not sure I'm ready yet,' she said, tucking in to the warm, tasty food.

The others had almost finished eating. The children were further along the big trestle table that took up most of the room. Flora waved to Oz and smiled. Oz felt really choked. The little girl reminded her so much of Katie. But she waved back and managed a rather watery smile.

Dave was on form, keeping the children amused.

'Which country has the best appetite?' he called out.

'I dunno,' giggled Flora.

'Hungary!'

'Ha ha!'

'When do astronauts eat?'

'We don't know.'

'At launch time!'

More laughter. Oz couldn't help joining in. Then, while she ate, she studied her new companions. Hazel and Rowan seemed to be great parents. The children were all chatting happily away, full of smiles and mischief. Mungo was dark and squat with a beard and bushy eyebrows. It turned out she was Hazel's brother. Holly was quite attractive with heaps of fair hair and dark blue eyes. Oz guessed she must be a few years older than her. She caught Holly's eye and smiled.

'It looks like we've got something in common,' said Holly. 'I ran away from home a few years ago.'

'Why?' asked Jo.

'I didn't get on with my parents,' said Holly. 'Simple as that.'

'Hey!' said Jo turning to Oz. 'Just like you.'

Oz nodded. She was rather glad that Jo was doing all the talking. She didn't trust herself to speak.

'Did you ever think of going home?' asked Jo.

'Did I?' said Holly with a sour look. 'Yes, I did! And I went. Once. For one miserable week.'

'What happened?' asked Jo.

'They pleaded with me to go back,' said Holly. 'Said they missed me.'

'Like yours,' Jo said to Oz.

Oz nodded again.

'I kept away for a bit,' said Holly. 'I wasn't going to grovel to them.'

'Sounds familiar,' said Jo.

'In the end I decided to go,' said Holly. 'Big mistake. They were even worse than before. Possessive. Domineering. Bullying. Spying on me all the time.'

'Oh,' said Oz.

'What have I said?' said Holly. 'Oz, you're looking a bit ghostly. Were you thinking of going home?'

Oz nodded.

'I'd think again,' said Holly. 'You might regret it.'

Oz was very quiet for the rest of the meal. What Holly had said had surprised her. She hadn't thought about what it might be like, how they might treat her if she went home. Perhaps it wasn't such a good idea after all.

The meal was over. Everyone helped clear away. Rowan produced a scrap of paper, held it up and grinned.

'This is the washing up rota,' he said.

Oz found she was first on the list. She had always hated washing up, but then she saw that her partner was Dave. He would snap her out of her doldrums. She didn't mind how many dishes were piled on the drainer if she could share the task with him.

'Right!' he said, wrapping his long arm round Oz's shoulder and grinning. 'Let's get at it.'

Oz hoped he would think the blush that rose to her face was because of the warm weather or the hot washing up water!

It didn't take them long and Oz felt so much more cheerful and rather smitten with Dave by the time they went to find the others who were ready for the evening picking.

They set off across the fields and were soon bending over the strawberry plants. Jim, their neighbour under the arches, had been right. Strawberry picking was a back-breaking job, but as Oz watched the sun setting behind the hill and stretched her aching body, she felt her unease melting away. It was so peaceful here. Why should she go home yet?

She had eaten a few delicious strawberries as she went along the rows, but most had ended up in the baskets. She had picked five baskets-full already. One by one she had taken them to the cart at the side of the field and they had been weighed and marked, then covered and piled with the others.

'These will be in the markets tomorrow,' said Mr Barnes.

That night, as Oz and Jo lay snuggled inside their sleeping bags, Jo whispered in the darkness.

'You like it here?'

'Yep,' said Oz, sleepily.

'We'll be here for a bit, won't we?'

'U-huh.'

'Not thinking of going home yet?'

'Not after what Holly said. That's put me off.'

'Good.'

'Why do you ask?' murmured Oz.

'I like having you around and … promise you won't laugh?'

'Cross my heart.' Oz was slowly drifting off to sleep.

'I think I'm in love,' said Jo.

Oz smiled to herself. Funny how they both seemed to have fallen for someone. 'Who's the lucky fella?' she murmured.

'Can't you guess?' whispered Jo. 'Dave, of course!'

When Oz had recovered from the surprise of Jo's confession, she turned over and tried to get to sleep. A few moments ago she couldn't keep awake. Now, her brain had become very active. So Jo had become her rival for Dave!

Don't be silly. You've only known him one day!

She thought about Jo. She was nice enough, but she was a bit quiet. Her nose was too pointed and she was so thin. Her hair was rather lanky and greasy. Hopefully, there was no way Dave would fall for her.

'Guess what,' she whispered. 'I fancy him, too.'

Jo giggled.

'Oh well,' she said. 'He probably doesn't like either of us.'

We'll see.

Chapter
TWELVE

The morning started early. The sun was hardly up and a cockerel was just beginning to crow noisily when a gong began to clang from the farmyard. Oz sat up and groaned. This was definitely the downside of the job. She yawned and stretched, then pulled herself out of her sleeping bag. She noticed Dave was not in his corner.

'Bags first shower,' she said and, grabbing her sponge bag, she opened the hut door and headed across the field.

Dave was just emerging from the showers.

'Sleep well?' asked Oz.

'My feather bed was much too soft,' said Dave cheerfully. 'And the servants hadn't ironed my pure silk sheets. But I managed.'

'About the same as me,' chuckled Oz. 'So what d'you make of the job, then?'

'Fabulous. I'm thinking of making it my lifelong occupation!'

Oz laughed and ran in for her shower. When she emerged a few minutes later, she found Dave sitting at the entrance of the hut talking to Jo. A sharp pang of jealousy shot through her. She hurried over and joined in the conversation. Then Jo left them and went for her shower.

At breakfast Oz forgot her jealousy when she realised how hungry she was. She helped herself to a plateful of bacon, sausages and eggs, a hunk of bread and a mug of tea. Jo sat beside her and they chatted all the way through breakfast. Jo was her mate, the best friend she had. She wasn't going to let a little thing like Dave come between them.

All through the long, hot day they knelt or bent double over the miles and miles of strawberry plants, filling basket after basket with the ripe fruit. Oz felt that her back would never straighten up and she was sure the red stains on her hands would never wash off!

Every now and then she took the basket to be weighed and counted by Mr Barnes. He was as morose as the night before. Oz wondered whether she could dare ask him for a small amount of her wages in advance. Holly's warning had made her think hard about going back, but she still wanted to phone home again soon. She spent a couple of hours plucking up courage to speak to the farmer. Eventually, she decided she had to do it.

'Mr Barnes,' she said, smiling as she handed over the next basket. 'How long will this job last?'

'Several weeks if the weather's kind to us,' said the farmer.

His surly expression didn't change. Oz almost gave up the attempt, but she managed to carry on.

'And when do we get paid?' she asked.

'At the end of the week,' said Mr Barnes, frowning. 'Why?'

'Well … '

'Spit it out, girl,' Mr Barnes said sharply. 'I won't bite your head off.'

'Well,' said Oz again. 'I was just wondering if there'd be any chance of a small advance?'

'Why?' He raised his eyebrows quizzically. 'Was it you who asked about the phone box?'

'Yes,' said Oz. 'And I'm absolutely skint and I wanted to make a call.'

Mr Barnes nodded.

'I don't see why not,' he said. 'You're a good worker. I can let you have a sub, if you like.'

Oz smiled up at him. 'That would be great.'

'Come to see me this evening, after you've eaten.'

'Thanks.'

Oz happily grabbed another basket and set off along the edge of the field towards the next row of strawberries. She was so deep in thought that she didn't notice the stranger leaning on the fence until he coughed loudly. Oz's heart somersaulted and she nearly dropped the basket.

'You gave me a fright,' she said, crossly.

She looked at him. He was quite tall, about Matt's age, she guessed, with steely blue eyes and bright ginger hair. Not her type at all. He looked tired and dirty. There was a black car parked nearby.

'Who's in charge here?' he asked.

Oz nodded her head in the direction of the farmer.

Then she turned her back on the stranger and found her place in the field.

'Who's that?' asked Jo.

'Dunno,' said Oz. 'I suppose he wants work.'

'Don't like the look of him.'

'Nor me. Let's hope Mr Barnes says no.'

But when Oz and Jo arrived back at the farm later in the day, tired and aching all over, they saw the black car parked at the edge of the yard and found the stranger in the far corner of the hut. He looked as if he had just had a shower. Oz wandered over to him.

'So he took you on, then?' she asked. 'What's your name?'

'Red.'

'Red? A funny sort of name.'

'It's the only one you're getting,' snapped Red.

'Ooh, touchy, aren't we?'

'I'm tired, that's all,' said Red. 'I've been on the road for days. I need to sleep.'

'I'm Oz,' said Oz.

'Well, that's rich,' said Red. 'And you thought I had the unusual name.'

Oz gave him a dirty look and went to eat. She was starving again.

'I don't know why I bothered to speak to that new bloke,' she said to Jo as they sat down. 'Talk about rude! And unfriendly. Another time I don't think I'll bother.'

'Not a patch on Dave!' said Jo.

'No,' said Oz, quietly.

At that moment, Red walked in. Everyone stopped talking and watched him help himself to a plate of food and sit down at the end of the table. He looked up and nodded at Mungo, who was nearest to him, but he didn't return Mungo's smile. Then he stared into his food and ignored everyone around him. He ate only a small amount then stood up, cleared away his plate and left.

'He's a right misery!' whispered Jo.

Oz nodded. She couldn't make out why Red was being so stand-offish. Still, it was none of her business.

As she wolfed her meal, she suddenly remembered what Mr Barnes had promised. Red's arrival had put it to the back of her mind. She quickly finished eating then, leaving Jo to do the washing up with Mungo, she went in search of the farmer.

She found him talking to Red. They were deep in

conversation, but stopped abruptly when Oz appeared. Very mysterious. Red ignored Oz and hurried away.

'Mr Barnes,' Oz said quietly as she watched Red disappear into the hut. 'Could I have a word, please?'

'What? Oh, yes,' he grunted. 'I hadn't forgotten. Come with me.'

Oz followed Mr Barnes to the farmhouse.

'Right,' he said at the door. 'How much do you need?'

'A couple of pounds, if that's all right.'

'No problem.'

He delved in his pocket and handed her three pound coins.

'Just in case you need more time,' he said. 'Good luck.'

Oz was amazed. The first pleasant remark he had made since they arrived. Dave had said that Mr Barnes wasn't as fierce as he seemed. She had proved him right.

'Thanks,' she said. 'You're very kind.'

She ran along the lane and soon arrived at the call box. Supposing her mum or dad answered. What was she going to say?

She stood for several minutes staring at the receiver, daring herself to pick it up and dial. Finally, holding her breath, she grabbed it and pushed a one pound coin into the slot. Then she punched out the number before she could change her mind.

Matt answered. Oz let out a rush of air.

'It's me again,' she said.

'Vick!' As before, Matt sounded really pleased to hear her.

'Thank goodness it's you,' she said. 'I don't think I can face Mum or Dad yet.'

'You still all right?'

'Yeah, fine.' She was in danger of blubbering again. 'I just thought I'd let you know I'm not in London any more.'

'Why? Where are you? On your way home?'

Matt's voice rose higher at each question. Was he really that excited at the prospect?

'No. I'm miles from nowhere, on a farm with a group of lovely people.'

'What? Now be careful, Vick. You don't know how vulnerable you are. Who are these people?'

Oz pushed a second coin in as the pips went. Then she told him about her new friends.

'And we're strawberry picking,' she said.

There was a pause.

'Mum's here,' said Matt. Oz heard him say something, but he had obviously put his hand over the receiver and she couldn't quite catch it. 'D'you want to speak to her?'

'No. Tell her I'm sorry, but I told you, I can't face her yet.'

'OK.'

Oz had had enough. 'Look, I have to go,' she said, hoping Matt hadn't noticed the flutter in her voice. She wanted to tell him that she missed them all, but she couldn't make the words come.

'Phone again soon,' said Matt.

Oz replaced the receiver and stepped outside the phone box. For a long time, she leaned against the glass and let the tears flow. Then she dried her eyes and set off for the farm.

Suddenly, she noticed Red standing nearby. He had his hands in his pockets and he was staring at her with a faraway expression in his eyes. Had he been there long? Had he followed her to the phone box? Was he spying on her?

Red took a step towards her and opened his mouth

to speak. Oz didn't wait to hear what he was going to say. She began to run back to the farm. It was a very lonely lane and she felt uneasy. Before she reached a bend in the lane, she quickly glanced back. Red had stepped into the phone box. She slowed down. Perhaps he hadn't followed her there, after all. He just wanted to use the phone.

For the next two days Oz hardly saw Red. He was only there in the mornings and evenings, but although he ate the same food and slept in the same hut, he said very little to anyone and never smiled. She couldn't put her finger on why he unnerved her so much. Maybe it was his sad blue eyes that always seemed to be watching.

The following afternoon, she was walking back from the strawberry field alone. The sun had become very hot and she needed to fetch a scarf to protect her head. She had left the field quite near the phone box. It was easier and quicker to reach the farm along the lane.

She had only been walking for a few seconds when she saw someone in the distance jogging towards her. He looked quite athletic. Then she realised, with surprise, that it was Red. He had the sun in his eyes and Oz didn't think he had seen her. She leapt up the bank at the side of the lane and hid behind a bush.

Red made for the phone booth and went in. Oz watched him dial, speak for barely a minute, put down the receiver and leave the box. Who had he phoned?

She remained hidden. She didn't feel like speaking to him. Anyway, it would seem very odd if she suddenly appeared out of the bushes. She watched him jog back towards the farm, then followed him at a distance.

What was he doing here? He went off in his black car every day. He had not been strawberry picking at all. He was a mystery.

Chapter
THIRTEEN

Red was just getting into his car when Oz reached the farm. He raised his hand as she hurried by on her way to the hut, but his eyes seemed to be looking right through her. Then he started the engine and the car sped away. As Oz delved in her rucksack, she puzzled over Red. He was unsociable, didn't talk to anyone except Mr Barnes, and didn't pick strawberries.

As soon as she returned to the field with her scarf, Oz told Jo about what she had witnessed.

'So what's he doing here?' Jo asked.

'Who knows!'

Red had a haunted look. Something was troubling him and Oz was determined to find out what it was. So when he returned later on, she tried to draw him into conversation, but he replied in the same curt manner and refused to look her in the eye. In the end, she gave up for the moment. She would try again later, catch him in a better mood. She still felt uneasy when he was around, yet something about him fascinated her.

But there was someone much more important and fascinating on the farm. Dave. Oz was just chatting to him when Holly dashed in.

'Come on, you two,' she panted. 'Have you forgotten? It's pay day.'

Oz felt a thrill of excitement as Mr Barnes handed over her pay packet – her first one ever! She ripped open the envelope and tipped out the contents. She counted the money. It would go a long way towards a train ticket. She would keep it safe until she had enough, just in case she decided she would go home after all.

During the next week, Red was hardly ever at the farm. He seemed to come and go as he pleased. Oz put her curiosity about him to one side and did all she could to win Dave over. She made him mugs of tea, smiled a lot when he was around, stayed near him whenever possible and started taking more care over her appearance. Then, one evening, she made up her face for the first time since her early days in London and took more than a few seconds to brush her hair.

Dave noticed!

'You look great,' he said with a flashing smile as they walked across from the hut for the evening meal.

Oz linked her arm through his. He didn't pull away.

'Fancy a walk afterwards?' he asked.

Oz's knees threatened to give way.

'Why not?' she said.

She couldn't eat much. Her stomach was too full of butterflies at the prospect of a walk alone with Dave. She wished he would hurry up and finish his. At last, he was ready.

'It's really good having you and Jo with us,' he said as they set off along the lane. 'And I've been waiting for a chance to talk to you.'

Oz was floating on air. He fancied her, too!

'I feel I can be honest with you, speak my mind,' he said.

Oz linked arms with him again and closed her eyes, letting him lead the way.

'It's about Jo,' said Dave.

Oz stopped dead, her eyes popped open.

'You what?'

'It's about Jo,' Dave repeated. 'That's what I wanted to talk to you about.'

Oz felt the warm glow fade and she slid down to earth with a bump.

'What about Jo?'

Dave grinned shyly. 'I wondered if you had any idea of my chances with her?'

Oz couldn't speak. She was totally deflated, devastated!

'Well? What d'you say?'

Oz turned and fled back towards the farm, her eyes streaming. She didn't care about the black mascara trails down her face. She cared about nothing. Dave didn't fancy her at all. He fancied Jo!

As she burst into the hut, she crashed into Red, almost knocking him over, but she hardly noticed.

She rushed to her rucksack and found Bruno.

'Why does everything have to go wrong?' she whispered between sobs.

Bruno stared back as usual. Oz heard footsteps on the wooden floor of the hut. It was Jo.

'Hey! What's up?' Jo's voice was full of concern.

How could Oz be angry with her? It wasn't her fault that Dave fancied her.

'You'd better hurry down the lane,' said Oz, wiping her eyes. 'There's someone waiting for you.'

'For me? Who?'

'Dave, of course. You're the one he's after.'

Jo sat down on the floor.

'Wow!' she said, and her face lit up.

'Go on,' said Oz. 'Don't make him change his mind.'

Jo didn't need any more persuasion. She leapt up and dashed for the door.

'Thanks, Oz,' she called as she left the hut.

Suddenly, Oz noticed that Red was staring at her from his dark corner of the hut. Had he been watching and listening all the time? She turned her back on him.

'Oz,' said Red, very quietly.

Oz was startled by the gentleness of his voice, but she didn't turn round.

'What?' she said.

'D'you want to talk?'

'*Me?* Talk to *you?*'

'Why not? I'm not an alien.'

'You might just as well be, though,' she said. 'Missing all day. Not fitting in with the rest. Not here to pick strawberries, that's for sure. So up to something else. What? A complete mystery.'

'I have my reasons.'

'Which are?'

'I'd rather not talk about it.'

'So why should I want to talk to you?'

'I thought … I wondered … I thought you seemed as if you needed to. You're unhappy.'

'Well, you're hardly a bundle of laughs,' said Oz.

'True.' Red's voice sounded sad.

Oz turned round at last. He was sitting cross-legged, facing her. So why was he interested in her? She stood up and walked slowly over to his corner.

'Why should you care?' she asked. 'I'm nothing to you.'

'True, but … '

He was still reluctant to give away any secrets. Oz found her old curiosity returning, so she sat down beside him.

'Well,' she said. 'How about I'll tell you about me, then you tell me about you? Is that a deal?'

'I'll think about it.'

They sat there in silence as the evening grew darker. Why did she feel so peaceful and relaxed, not at all how she had felt before when he was around? Maybe he would turn out to be nice. She was gradually beginning to realise that, in a funny sort of way, she quite liked him.

'All right,' he agreed at last.

It was almost dark. Red was in shadow. All Oz could see of him were his pale, freckled face and his steely eyes. She might as well confide in him. There couldn't be any harm in it.

'I suppose you're right,' she said. 'I do need to talk. I think I must be missing my brother, Matt. Not that we'd been getting on all that well.'

'So you've got a family?'

'Yes.'

'A brother. Who else?'

'A little sister, Katie.'

'What's she like?'

'Oh, she's only four. Spoilt. You know.'

'And they've both been getting up your nose?'

'You got it in one.'

'Bad enough to make you leave home?'

When Oz heard it put like that, I seemed a very petty reason to run away.

'But it wasn't just Matt and Katie,' she said. 'It was Mum and Dad, mostly Dad. I told him I hated him.'

'And do you?'

Oz shrugged. She was silent for a while. How could she say she hated her dad?

'No,' she said.

She had poured out her troubles before, to Lizzie and Uncle Tom, Paul and Jo, but somehow, telling Red, her problems seemed much less terrible.

'Maybe I shouldn't have been quite so revolting! I reckon I hardly gave them an easy time.'

'Do you regret running away?'

Oz shrugged. How could she answer that with a yes or no? Of course, there had been many utterly miserable days and some terrifying moments on the streets, but she had met some really great people and now she was enjoying herself here on the farm. And it was fantastic to get a wage packet at the end of each week.

'Yes *and* no,' she said. 'I admit I miss them, but … '

'Did you phone them the other day? Is that why you were crying at the phone box?' His voice had a kind, sad tone.

Oz nodded in the darkness. Yet again, the thought of home made her fill up with tears. Red didn't speak for a while, but reached out and took her hand. She didn't pull away. 'And will you ever go home?' he asked.

Oz was just beginning to nod again when there were voices and laughter outside and Jo and Dave burst into the hut. Jo flicked the light switch. Oz was dazzled by the sudden brilliance. She blinked and shaded her eyes.

'Hey!' shouted Jo. 'What's going on here?'

'Nothing,' said Oz.

'Nothing?' laughed Dave. 'Sitting here in pitch darkness holding hands. You're a quick worker, Oz, I'll say that for you.'

Oz leapt up, angry.

'Mind your own business!' she shouted and stormed out of the hut.

She marched round the farm buildings, trying to burn off her anger.

Trust Jo to misunderstand what was going on! Trust Dave to laugh at everything!

Hazel was sitting on the steps of her caravan as Oz hurried by.

'All right, Oz?' she called.

'U-huh,' Oz muttered.

She didn't want to get involved in talking with anyone else. Maybe she had said too much to Red. Then it occurred to her. He hadn't kept his side of the bargain. She still didn't know his story.

Chapter
FOURTEEN

When Oz woke, she noticed immediately that Red was not in his corner of the hut. She sat up and gasped. His bedding was gone. Had he left the farm for good? What a dirty cheat, after making her confide in him. So much for his promise to reveal his own secrets.

Jo, Holly and Dave were still asleep. Oz quickly pulled on her clothes and hurried outside. It was raining, the first rain since they had arrived here. Hazel was just leaving the showers with the three children in tow. Flora rushed over and wrapped her arms round Oz. Oz smiled and hugged her back.

'Feeling better this morning?' called Hazel.

'Yes, thanks.' It was easier than telling the truth. She didn't feel any better. She had been annoyed with Jo and Dave last night, but it wasn't that. She had enjoyed those few minutes with Red more than she wanted to admit, so today she felt let down.

'I'm not sure if we'll be picking today in this weather,' said Hazel. 'Come and have a cuppa with us later. And play with the kids.'

'OK,' said Oz, though she didn't feel very sociable.

She ran across the farmyard towards the area where Red parked his car. If she couldn't find the car, it would mean he had definitely left. There was no car. Red had gone.

Thoroughly fed up, Oz wandered slowly around the farm. She didn't notice that she was wet through until she met Jo emerging from the hut.

'Where've you been?' cried Jo, grabbing Oz's arm and pulling her inside. 'I thought you'd deserted me because I upset you last night.'

'No,' said Oz, with a smile. 'I've been for a walk.'

'In this?'

Jo handed Oz her towel. Oz pointed to the empty space where Red's belongings had been and shrugged her shoulders.

'Oh,' said Jo. 'He's gone.'

Oz nodded then rubbed her hair dry and changed her clothes.

'Where's Dave?' she asked.

'Shower.'

'So,' said Oz. 'Do I detect romance in the air?'

Jo blushed. 'I'd never have thought he'd fall for plain old me,' she said. 'He's lovely.'

Oz didn't feel jealousy now. After all, she hadn't really been in love with Dave. She hadn't known him long enough. And Jo was such a sweet person. She deserved a bit of luck.

'Let's go and have breakfast,' she said.

Dave bounded in and kissed Jo. Jo's eyes shone and she looked pretty. Oz was happy for her.

Over breakfast, Oz explained about Red.

'And finding us holding hands,' she said. 'That was nothing. He was just trying to comfort me, that's all.'

'He's a real odd one,' said Jo. 'I wonder what made him scarper like that.'

'There's something getting to him,' said Oz. 'He was very cagey last night, but I'd just about persuaded him to tell me about himself when you love birds burst in and ruined it.'

'Oh,' said Jo. 'Sorry.'

'Maybe I'll never know now,' said Oz. She wished she wasn't left with such a strong feeling of disappointment.

Hazel's prediction was right. There was no picking that morning, so Oz smothered her feelings and spent much of the time playing with Tinkerbell, Flora and Silvan. It was incredible how much Flora reminded her of Katie.

'You like children, don't you?' Hazel said.

Oz nodded. She amazed herself. She would never have thought that. Not after how she used to feel about Katie.

By lunchtime, the rain had eased off. The sun came out and a drying wind blew across the fields. Mr Barnes appeared.

'Time to pick more strawberries,' he said. 'We have to get them in quickly now they're wet, or they'll rot.'

The novelty had worn off. If it weren't for the prospect of money, Oz might have tried to get out of going to the fields. She felt tired and depressed. Perhaps she could phone home later. She could afford it now.

That afternoon, just before everyone headed back to the farm, Oz slipped off to the phone box, hoping that Matt would answer again. But she heard her mum's voice on the other end of the phone. She gripped the receiver tightly and gritted her teeth. Could she cope with talking to her mum?

'Hello? Hello?' said Mum. Then she spoke to someone else. 'There's nobody there. Do you think it could be Vicky?'

There was a rustling noise.

'Vicky, is that you?' It was her dad!

Oz wanted the ground to swallow her. This was worse! How could she speak to *him*?

'Vicky? If it's you, speak, will you? Tell us you're all right.' He didn't sound fierce or angry. His voice was shaking with emotion.

Oz heard the same rustling noise.

'Please come home soon,' pleaded her mum. 'We all miss you so much.'

Oz swallowed hard. It was becoming difficult not to give in, especially when her mum started to cry.

'We'll try and understand,' her mum sobbed. 'If only you'll come home.'

Oz remembered Holly's warning. But her mum wasn't like that.

She took a deep breath. 'Hi, Mum,' she said.

It was very difficult, listening to what her mum had to say. About how much Katie loved her and how they had involved the police and homeless charities and other agencies to help find her. How they had all searched in London. It was a relief when the pips sounded.

'I have to go,' said Oz, thankful that the ordeal was almost over. 'I promise I'll ring again soon.'

'But, Vicky,' pleaded Mum. 'Why don't you tell us where you are and we'll come and get you?'

'No, Mum,' said Oz. 'I have to … '

The phone went dead and Oz returned to the farm in a dream. She stood quietly, waiting her turn for her wages. She counted the money. Another week's earnings should be enough for her fare. If she could face it!

Darkness came suddenly, as the black clouds returned.

'I think I'll turn in early,' Oz said to Jo and Holly after they had finished eating.

'But it's only eight o'clock,' said Jo.

'I know, but I'm tired.'

'OK,' said Jo. 'We'll try not to disturb you when we come in.'

As Oz got ready for bed, she could hear the chattering of her new friends as they sat near the caravans round a small camp fire. She heard laughter and singing. Everyone sounded so happy, but she didn't feel in the mood to join them. She needed to be on her own.

Then, over the sound of voices, Oz heard a car. It stopped in the farm. Two doors slammed. Who was visiting the farm at this time of night?

Everyone was silent for a few seconds, then they all started talking at once. Who was it? What was going on?

Footsteps sounded outside the hut, then the door opened. Red stood in the doorway. But not the Red she would recognise. This one was grinning from ear to ear and he was not alone. From behind him stepped a girl, shorter than him and probably younger than Oz, but the likeness was striking. She had the same steely blue eyes and red hair.

'This is my sister, Lucy,' said Red.

Chapter
FIFTEEN

Red led Lucy into the hut and brought her over to Oz.

'Hi,' said Oz, smiling at Lucy, who seemed dazed and nervous. She was shivering and had dark rings round her eyes. She looked as if she had been crying.

Oz handed her a blanket and Red gently wrapped it round her shoulders. Lucy and Red sat down on the floor beside Oz.

'You must have been wondering about me,' he said.

'You did the dirty on me, disappearing like that,' said Oz, frowning, although she was bursting to tell him how glad she was to see him.

'I'm sorry,' said Red.

'Why did you persuade me to confide in you if you were about to vanish?'

'I didn't know I was,' said Red. 'It was as much a surprise to me as it was to you.'

'And you'd promised to tell me your problems,' said Oz. 'I thought you must have chickened out.'

'It wasn't like that.'

Lucy lay down and snuggled into the blanket. Almost immediately, she was asleep. Red fetched another blanket to cover her then he sat down close to Oz.

'I think I owe you an explanation,' he said quietly.

Oz nodded.

'Lucy's only fourteen,' said Red. 'When our dad died about a year ago, she took it terribly badly. It was extremely sudden and they had been very close.'

Oz glanced at Lucy, who looked peaceful and childlike in her sleep.

'Somehow, she couldn't accept that he was dead. She went totally weird. Wouldn't speak, didn't eat. She was under the doctor and a psychiatrist, even a hypnotherapist, but nobody could snap her out of her trauma.'

'Poor thing,' said Oz.

'Then one day she went missing. Didn't leave a note like you did, but we presumed that she had gone to look for Dad. We had no idea where she had gone and no amount of searching could find her.'

'Is that why you were interested in my story?'

'Yes, I suppose so. Anyway, when she disappeared, I'd been at Uni a couple of years and Mum rang me in a dreadful state. I zoomed straight home. Luckily, it was almost the end of my term. I'd just finished my exams. Mum doesn't drive, so it was down to me to do all the long-distance searching. I've followed lead after lead. People reported seeing her – she's distinctive with that bright red hair … '

He smiled at Oz as she raised her eyes to his matching hair.

' … but each time I arrived, she'd gone.'

'So why this farm? Has she been here?'

'Not exactly, but years ago, my dad was at college with Mr Barnes, so he was one of the people we phoned. We were desperate, so we tried everyone we could think of. Anyway, quite recently, he rang Mum back. He told her that he had been asking around and a man he knows had seen a girl that could be her. Mr Barnes said I could base myself here on his farm and travel round.'

Things were becoming clearer to Oz. That's why he didn't pick strawberries, and why he disappeared each day, and why he seemed friendly with the farmer.

'But why did you keep all this to yourself?' she asked.

'I don't know,' said Red. 'I've been a total zombie since this happened. Maybe I'm cracking up, too. You must have thought I was so rude.'

Oz smiled. She wasn't going to deny it.

'Anyway, very early this morning, Mr Barnes came rushing over. He'd had a call from another farmer friend. Someone fitting Lucy's description had turned up. I didn't waste any time. I packed my bags and crept out.'

'And you found her!' said Oz.

'Yes, eventually. About four o'clock this afternoon. She was huddled in a barn on a farm about twenty miles away, cold, hungry and terrified.'

'Was she pleased to see you?'

'Was she? She flung her arms round my neck and sobbed. I hope that's done her good. She wasn't able to cry when Dad died.'

'I'm glad you found her,' said Oz, touching Red's hand.

'So am I,' said Red, his eyes warm and contented. 'The understatement of the millennium!'

'Have you rung your mum?'

'Of course I have. I was under strict instructions to let her know immediately there was some news. I've been ringing her every day. Funny that we should both be using that phone box, Oz. I'm glad it was there. Stupid of me, but I lost my mobile.'

'Mine's got a flat battery!' Oz smiled. 'Are you on your way home now?'

Red nodded.

'Thanks for coming to tell me,' said Oz.

'I wanted to keep last night's promise,' said Red. 'But that's not the only reason I came back. I wanted to see you and I wanted to try and persuade you to go home, too.'

Oz's eyes filled with tears. Even after all he had gone through to find his own sister, he still had concern for her.

'Thanks,' she whispered. She leaned over and kissed his cheek. 'How far have you got to drive? Where do you live?'

When she heard where he and Lucy came from, she gasped.

'I don't believe it!' she cried. 'That's only ten miles from my home.'

Lucy sat up, staring around her like a startled animal.

'It's all right, Luce,' said Red, putting his arm round her. 'You're safe now. Remember, we're on our way home.'

Lucy nodded. There was a slight smile in her eyes.

'Oz,' said Red.

'What?'

'We'll give you a lift if you like.'

It was rather sudden. Did she have to make a decision now? Could she face it?

'Come on,' said Red. 'You know you're desperate to go home.'

Oz looked at Lucy. The sleep had done her good. She wasn't looking so haunted now. Her brother had come to find her.

She thought of Matt. He had tried to find her, too. And she had enjoyed talking to him on the phone. Why not? Surely Mum and Dad weren't such ogres. They'd be all right.

'OK,' she said. 'Give me ten minutes.'

Ten minutes wasn't long to pack Matt's rucksack, to explain her departure to Mr Barnes, to thank the group of people who had brought her out of London, to hug the children and finally to say a tearful goodbye to Jo.

'Don't worry about me,' said Jo, her eyes streaming. 'Dave will look after me, won't you, Dave?'

'Not if my presence makes you cry so much,' laughed Dave, wiping her eyes.

'I'll let you know how I get on,' said Oz, giving Jo one last hug.

Lucy fell asleep again as soon as the car headed away from the farm, but Oz was wide awake. Now she had made the decision, she felt excited, nervous. Would it really be all right?

She and Red talked all the way, along busy motorways and quieter roads. By the time they reached the familiar streets of her town, Oz felt she was getting to know him quite well. And she discovered that she was growing quite fond of him. She listened to his voice and knew she liked the sound of it. It was a pity they had to say goodbye after just starting to get to know each other.

In a mixture of excitement, nervousness and regret, she directed him to her house and he stopped the car outside. It was very late, but there was a light on in her mum and dad's bedroom.

'Keep in touch,' said Red, as he lifted the rucksack from the boot.

Oz nodded. She felt tearful again. She stepped forward to kiss Red and he returned the kiss.

'Here, take this,' he said, thrusting a piece of paper into her hand. 'Please, keep in touch.'

Oz heaved the rucksack on to her back and hurried to the door, waving as the car sped off along the road. She stared at the front door, remembering those times when she had arrived home late. That all seemed a lifetime ago!

With shaking hands she reached out and rang the bell. Part of her wanted to run away, but it was too late now. She stood shivering on the doorstep, listening to voices inside and the sound of people coming downstairs.

She was dragged inside, not with anger this time, but with hugs and tears. They made so much noise that first Matt then Katie woke up and rushed downstairs. Matt's arms almost crushed her, then she picked up Katie and hugged her tightly. How she had missed them both!

And as Oz looked at her mum and dad and Matt and Katie, she didn't regret coming back. Maybe they would have to work at it, but she knew it was going to be all right.

Suddenly, she remembered the piece of paper Red had given her. It was screwed up tightly in her hand. She opened it out. It was a phone number.

'Keep in touch,' he had said.

He wasn't at all like the first impression she and Jo had had of him. He had shown he was kind and gentle and he wanted to see her again. And she knew that she wanted very much to carry on seeing Red.